Wagon, Chariot and Carriage

STUART PIGGOTT

Wagon, Chariot and Carriage

SYMBOL AND STATUS
IN THE HISTORY OF TRANSPORT

WITH 33 ILLUSTRATIONS

THAMES AND HUDSON

© 1992 Thames and Hudson Ltd

First published in the United States in 1992 by Thames and Hudson Inc., 500 Fifth Avenue, New York, New York 10110

Library of Congress Catalog Card Number 92-70866

Printed and bound in Slovenia

Contents

PRINCELY GIFT · HORSES AS GODS AND SACRIFICES · THE
SACRIFICIAL HORSE · HORSE BURIALS IN PREHISTORY · EARLY
MEDIEVAL EUROPE · HORSE AND SHAMAN · HORSES FOR PARADISE

FROM CHARIOT TO PLEASURE-CAR IN THE ANCIENT EAST · THE
PAZYRYK CEREMONIAL CARRIAGE · WAGON AND CARRIAGE IN THE
WEST · THE PIVOTED FRONT AXLE FROM PREHISTORY TO
HISTORY · TILT-WAGONS AND CARTS IN ANTIQUITY · THE
MEDIEVAL COVERED PLEASURE CARRIAGE · FROM TILT-CARRIAGE
TO COACH · THE COACH ACCEPTED · THE COACH AS PRESTIGE
GIFT: ELIZABETH AND RUSSIA · THE INDIAN GIFT: JAMES I AND
JAHANGIR · COACHES TO CHINA: THE GREAT
INCOMPATIBILITY · THE END: THE GLAMOUR OF ANACHRONISM

Preface

In writing this book I have drawn heavily on my own previous study, *The Earliest Wheeled Transport* (1983), bringing this up to date where necessary. I gratefully acknowledge the help I have received from colleagues and friends, to one of whom, Mrs Mary Littauer, I owe more than formal gratitude for her constant help and encouragement over many years, though I would not implicate her in any conclusions I may have drawn. In addition, my thanks for personal assistance go to Miss Janet Backhouse, Professor Sandor Bökönyi, Professor John Crook, Professor Joost Crouwel, the late Professor R.H.C. Davis, Dr Arthur MacGregor, Dr Andrew Sherratt, Dr Ian Stead, Mr Michael Strachan and Professor Charles Thomas. Throughout I have been aided and supported by the devoted and critical help of Ruth Daniel and the editorial staff of Thames and Hudson.

West Challow July 1991

1 Representation of wagon and horses on cinerary urn, Hallstatt C/D, Sopron, Hungary.

Introduction

This book comprises a group of essays forming studies in pomp and circumstance in the regal and noble transport by vehicle or steed in antiquity, stressing two main themes: the continuity of prehistory and history, and the constant interaction between east and west in the Old World, between the Orient and western Europe. It is essentially a personal book in its selection and emphasis. The art historian Fritz Saxl once wrote that he saw himself as 'a labourer tilling the soil on the border strip' between more than one academic discipline and added, 'I have almost always enjoyed this life.' I would endorse Saxl's two comments for my own approach to the past, and more particularly in the present essays on the means whereby magnificence was achieved and maintained on steed or vehicle. When this book was being planned a discerning critic groaned wearily 'Not *another* book about horses?' Though Equids are at many points discussed, the writer is no hippophile and his comments are made with disinterested detachment. I would claim alliance rather with Edward Gibbon, who in his autobiography records that, reconciled to a sedentary life, 'the horse, the favourite of my countrymen, never contributed to the pleasures of my youth.'

A final general point may be made in passing. Although sentiment (or sentimentality) in some quarters today finds it repugnant to admit, early people as the domesticators of the draught animals of antiquity, cattle and equids, must be seen as predators in competition with others, even after the cultivation of the first cereal crops. With fields of crops the necessity of fencing herds in is no less important than fencing out the wild herbivores as potential crop robbers. And it is not always recognized that large predators had a surprisingly long survival in the ancient Near East and Europe.[1] The range of the wolf and bear into historic times extended as far south as the Levant, where also a species of lion lived in Syria, Mesopotamia, Persia and the Caucasus and even Europe, in southern Thrace south of the Rhodope and east of the Pindus. Herodotus has a vivid account of the attack here by mountain lions on the camels of the army of

Xerxes in 480 BC. 'The whole region is full of lions and wild bulls with gigantic horns' he wrote (*Histories* VII, 125–126), and the lions are later confirmed by Aristotle and the elder Pliny. Lions and the lion hunt after all formed subjects for Mycenaean art;[2] snow leopards appear in the Caucasus on metalwork from the third millennium BC, the artistic motif of a deer attacked by a large feline is a commonplace of Scythian art, and lions, tigers and leopards appear at Pazyryk in the fifth century BC. The Hebrew poet of the eighth century BC neatly paired predators and prey in his millenarian vision –

The wolf also shall dwell with the lamb, and the leopard shall lie down with the kid, and the calf and the young lion and the fatling together, and the cow and the bear shall feed...(Isaiah 11, 6–7)

In general, after touching on the recurrent phenomenon of innovating and conserving societies in antiquity, I have followed a chronological sequence, allowing myself from time to time to pursue the archaeology of related issues not strictly part of the main narrative, such as the relationship of chariotry to the speakers of early Indo-European languages in Chapter II, or in Chapter III the interaction between horse riding and the changing modes of men's clothing in classical and early medieval times.

Chapter I opens with a discussion of the first circumstances of the use in prehistory of animals, first oxen and later equids, for traction or other secondary uses beyond the simple supply of fresh meat. Here the ox-wagon takes priority with its early adoption as a prestige burial carriage and its ultimate appearance as the archaic royal conveyance of the early Merovingian kings. In Chapter II we come to the first use of equids for draught, especially the horse in conjunction with the new invention of the light spoked-wheeled chariot. A discussion follows on the distinction between sporadic barbarian chariot-using and the institutionalized chariotry of the ancient civilized states including China. Here an excursus into Indo-European linguistic affiliations becomes necessary.

By Chapter III we find the chariot in decline as a vehicle of prestige and its replacement by the horse as the steed of majesty and nobility. Another side-issue is taken up, the changes in clothing and armour styles among horsemen in the Orient and western Europe from late prehistory through the classical period into the Middle Ages. Finally the records of pagan horse-worship and sacrifice in early medieval Europe and the Asiatic steppe by western travellers from Herodotus to the high Middle Ages are set out. Here too the plausibility of an underlying element of shamanism is suggested. Since writing this part of the book my attention has been drawn to a possible parallel from the New World, where the American Indians have long been associated with elements of shamanism of northeast Asiatic derivation. A platform burial of the Crow Indians, set up recently enough to be photographed, shows below the corpse the heads and tails of a pair of his horses, in a manner strikingly similar to other contemporary early photographs of horse-hide sacrifices in Central Asia.[3]

The final chapter brings to a close the pursuit of vehicles and steeds of majesty and prestige with the medieval development of the covered carriage as an invention sponsored by high-ranking ladies (and the higher clergy) to achieve some element of comfort in formal travel, and the subsequent establishment of the coach as an archaism cherished today among other features of re-invented tradition of royal display.

I

The Ox-Wagon from the Farmyard to the Court

By around 6000 BC, several human communities in Western Asia, and very little later Europe, had achieved an economic status with a stable foundation in what constituted the basic prerequisites of mixed farming: the cultivation of a cereal crop and the domestication of more than one species of mammal, thus ensuring a balanced diet of proteins and carbohydrates. Among these from the first had been, together with the pigs and ovicaprids (sheep and goats), the larger and more powerful cattle, to be joined, from about 4000 BC, by horses. (The English language has no singular noun including bull and cow, though a horse may be a stallion or a mare: an ox is technically a castrated bull, though the word is often loosely used to denote any domestic bovid.) The distinction of the larger animal domesticates in Eurasia as against the Americas is of importance when we come, as we now do, to their use for draught: the New World could offer as domesticates only the small camelids such as the llama or vicuna for such purposes – guinea pigs and turkeys were clearly not in the running.

Our understanding of Old World animal management after the initial provision of a captive meat supply was put on a new footing by Andrew Sherratt's now classic study of 1981.[1] Here he demonstrated that the recognition of a range of 'secondary' uses became apparent to a number of population groups, either technologically stone-using ('Neolithic') or with incipient non-ferrous metallurgy ('Early Bronze Age'), at a surprisingly consistent date, about 3500 BC or a little earlier, and certainly demonstrated archaeologically as a new technological complex in the half millennium 3500–3000 BC. These 'secondary products' included wool for fabrics (cloth or felt) from sheep and goats, milk as a food component (including cheese, yoghurt and the fermented *kumis*) from cows, ewes, goats and mares, and, most important in the present context, traction for plough and transport. Here the primary choice was obviously enough the largest and most powerful domesticate, cattle. Here too, the initial selection from the wild would have been the smaller and more docile individuals, and domestication brought with it a diminution in size. The wild *Bos primigenius* averaged a withers height of up to 170 cm (17 hands, 5 ft 10 in) for bulls and 150–155 cm for cows: domestic cattle by the fourth millennium BC in Europe and the Near East ranged from 140 to 120 cm. Potential draught would have to be provided by beasts of around 13 hands, and this factor may have played a part in oxen being used for traction in pairs, as the evidence shows from the beginning.

The traction plough as a component of the 'secondary products' complex of animal exploitation does not concern us here, and can be seen less as a technological innovation than as an adaptation of already existing hoes for manual cultivation. But the two- or four-wheeled vehicle, cart or wagon is a complete innovation and in itself a complex piece of technology which justifies the popular phrase 'a new invention'. Before going on with our main theme – the degree to which this innovation came to acquire prestige and status beyond its basic function – two general points are worth making. In the first place we come up against another cliché, 'the invention of the wheel'. This embodies a number of misconceptions about the history of technology in antiquity, the first being the assumption that practical developments are necessarily the concrete expressions of a generalizing abstract concept, in this case of rotary motion, in which the use of wheels to minimize the friction between a load and the ground over which it is being dragged is seen as being directly ancestral to the rotating weight of the distaff spindle or the potter's free-moving moulding board, the rotary mill powered by animals, water or wind; gears, ratios, transverse drive and crank-shafts; clockwork and steam and petrol engines. The history of the earliest technology does not support such a view: both spindle whorl and potter's wheel are devices for maintaining the momentum of a spinning vertical shaft, the first antecedent to wheeled transport, the second in no way coincident in time or space. We have, therefore, to deal with an innovation and an invention of profound potential to civilization, but not with the discovery of an abstract truth in mechanics.

The second point to be made is one which concerns all technological innovations in relation to human communities: the value attached to a new invention within the social setting in which it is contained.

It is a very simplistic idea that what is to us 'useful' will be thought so and immediately utilized by everyone else. The real problem seems first to have been recognized for what it is by the great historian Marc Bloch, in a paper to a conference of psychologists in 1941, though not accessibly published until after his death, in 1966. He remarks:

Let us suppose that there has been some new technique, either invented within a given society, or introduced from outside. It will sometimes be accepted by that society, and sometimes rejected. What causes lie behind these varying reactions?... One idea comes first to mind. The invention will be accepted if it is, or appears to be, useful, and rejected if apparently useless or danger-ous... But we are soon led to feel that matters are not quite so simple or so rational... we have a very clear impression that some societies are in themselves more 'routine-minded' and others more 'accustomed to change'.[2]

Unaware at that time of Bloch's ideas, in 1955 I wrote of prehistory that I seemed to perceive:

a broad classification between *innovating* and *conserving* societies. In the one group technological developments in the arts of war and peace must have been socially acceptable and therefore encouraged; in the other, once a satisfactory *modus vivendi* for the community has been achieved, there seems no urgent need to alter the situation.[3]

As the ultimate heirs of the innovators of antiquity, we tend to regard technological developments as on the whole desirable, inevitable, and bound up with woolly beliefs about 'progress'. But like Bloch I feel that it is 'not quite so simple or so rational' as all that. As Sir Moses Finley later put it, 'Economic growth, technical progress, increasing efficiency are not "natural" virtues; they have not always been possibilities or even desiderata.'[4] In the history of wheeled transport we have an almost universal situation of ready acceptance and innovation in a diverse series of societies over a varied and extensive geographical area, though two great civilizations of antiquity, Egypt and China, only adopted wheeled transport at a comparatively late date and in the form of the horse-drawn chariot, the one in the seventeenth, the other in the twelfth century BC. And we should also remember how in the New World a knowledge of movement on wheels, independent of outside influences, was never exploited beyond little pottery toys, and that in the Old World, a large part of the late antique, and later Islamic, world between the third and seventh centuries AD, abandoned wheeled transport in favour of camels for riding or as pack animals.[5]

Clearly then the whole complex of Sherratt's 'secondary products' exploitation developed in a briskly innovative social climate, and nowhere is this more apparent than in the wheeled vehicles drawn by oxen which are now our immediate concern.[6] But before the wagon, the sledge.

From sledge to wheels

The earliest devices for minimizing friction between a dragged load and the ground were sledges (and for personal use in snowy landscapes, skis). Wooden composite sledges were used by early hunter-fisher societies in near-Arctic northern Europe by 7000 BC at least: dog traction is assumed but not directly attested. But a sledge does not need snow, and is equally useful on the dry grass of the steppe, where its use around 4000 BC is shown by pottery models of sledges, one on log-runners and one on edge-on planks, from sites of the Tripolye culture of South Russia. So too on the arid ground of Mesopotamia, where it has long been recognized that the earliest representations of vehicles, in the pictographic script of the late fourth millennium BC, include both sledges and sledge-bodies on wheels. Of the same date is a carved stone plaque showing 'an important personage (or conceivably, the effigy of a deity) seated in a litter with an arched tilt, the legs of which are set on such a sledge' as in the pictographs, and drawn by oxen. Here, from the first, is a sledge of prestige, and indeed rather later, in the mid third millennium BC, an actual 'sledge throne' was placed in the tomb of Queen Pu-abi in the royal cemetery of Early Dynastic Ur.[7] A vehicle buried with the dead can only be interpreted in terms of status and prestige, shared by the vehicle and its deceased owner, and the Mesopotamian circumstances are repeated on the South Russian steppe at about the same time, around 3000–2500 BC by the burial with a sledge in a grave of the Pit Grave culture at Kholmskoe near Odessa, a light structure 1.8 m long.[8] Burials with wheeled vehicles are, as we shall shortly see, frequent in the Pit Grave and allied tombs from the Danube to the Volga and again must surely be status symbols, yet away in Britain at Dorchester-on-Thames, in a wholly different archaeological context of mid-third-millennium date, a sledge-burial repeats the same symbolism. Even before the technological advent of wheeled transport, the prestige of ox-traction for the personage of distinction established itself, and with the wagon and the cart, they came from their beginnings to rise in the social scale from farm vehicles to upper-class carriages. To them we may now turn.

Technology and its constraints

Like a sledge, a wagon (four-wheeled) or a cart (two-wheeled) is a piece of carpentry demanding adequate timber as raw material, and above all wood for the solid disc wheels which abundant archaeological evidence shows to have been universal before the invention of the spoked wheel, with its distinctively different technology, in the second millennium BC, and associated with equid traction. I discussed disc wheel construction in 1983 and here a brief account of the factors involved in the first vehicle construction will be sufficient.

In the first place, adequate heavy timber supplies are essential which, if a single area of origin were to be sought, would preclude open steppe or semi-desert conditions which do not support the requisite botanical species.[9] The single-piece disc wheels of the early third millennium BC in northwest Europe, averaging 80 cm in diameter, were cut out of tangential or chord-split planks from oak or alder stems at least 1.0 m thick, and therefore from trees 200–300 years old. Even the three-piece wheel made from morticed planks, so early devised, in a way which halves the width of the initial requirement, makes heavy demands on adult timber. That such massive planks were obtained in antiquity is shown by many finds other than wheels, the most striking of recently discovered examples being those of the burial chamber of the Haddenham long barrow in the Cambridge Fens, tangentially split with stone tools from a 300–400-year-old tree up to 1.5 m in diameter, and dating to 4000–3500 BC.[10] Trees of such age and diameter in natural stands of broad-leaved hard-woods are estimated by botanists to average not more than seven to the hectare, and the required planks and the subsequent heavy carpentry were achieved, outside the ancient Near East, with stone tools. The whole enterprise of building an ox-wagon in the early stages of secondary exploitation of tractive power was one demanding a considerable expenditure of the skills of craftsmen, from lumberjacks to joiners, and the result was inevitably a ponderous vehicle. The parent plank of one of the Dutch disc wheels of the third millennium BC would have weighed 322 kg, and a complete four-wheeled wagon would have a weight of not less than about 670–700 kg (two-thirds of a ton). This is twenty times the weight of a modern replica of an ancient Egyptian chariot of the mid-second millennium BC (34 kg) and underlines the necessity of employing a pair of oxen for its traction, which would be slow at the best of times: some 3.2 km per hour as against chariot horses at 10–14 km at a trot, 20–30 km at a gallop. Speed was not a glamorous component of the early prestige of ox traction.

Constructionally the first wheeled vehicles consisted of one or two pairs of wheels with their axles, either both turning together or with the axle fixed and the wheels rotating freely upon it. On one or two of these units was set the body or box of the cart or wagon. The disc wheels were either single-piece or composite, normally of three morticed planks, the central one bearing the hub or nave twice the width of the others, thereby economizing by a factor of one half in the width of the parent tangential plank. This tripartite, and so more sophisticated, type, is known from the Rhine to the Indus by around 3000 BC: in Switzerland in the local stone-using cultures between 3500 and 3000 BC and in the Harappa civilization with copper and bronze metallurgy by about 2500 BC, thus arguing for the adoption of a common technological tradition unrelated to other cultural or social boundaries. Harnessing the pair of draught oxen was by a central pole with a yoke either bearing on the withers or attached to the horns. When horses first came to be used in their turn for draught, this form of yoke harnessing was to persist with little modification, though it was unsuitable to the equine anatomy and reduced the animal's traction force. But it continued until the development of the rigid collar and shafts first in China by the third to fifth centuries AD, and in western Europe not effectively until about AD 800.

The first ox-wagons: function and status

We are now in a position to consider the archaeological evidence for the earliest wheeled vehicles, whether actual surviving finds of wagons or their wheels, or representations in pictorial or model form.[11] We have already touched on the 'vehicle' signs in the pictographic script of Uruk IV in late fourth-millennium BC Mesopotamia, and of similar or rather earlier date are the remains of an actual wagon, in the form of an axle-and-wheels unit, and another wheel, in a late Neolithic settlement site at Zürich in Switzerland. These wheels are of composite tripartite construction, and north-west European finds of single-piece disc wheels from Holland and

Denmark date from early in the third millennium BC. The Zürich wagon was literally stuck in the mud of a settlement, and other Swiss finds, and the Dutch and Danish examples, seem utilitarian enough, though some might have been votive offerings.

When we turn to the late fourth-millennium evidence from central and eastern Europe we seem to encounter the wagon in another social context, that of ritual and burial. We may begin with two cups of fine pottery from graves in Hungary at Budakalász and Szigetszentmárton in Hungary, of the local Baden culture, between 3500 and 3000 BC, which are accurately modelled in the form of wagons with four disc wheels; another pottery model of the same date from Radošina in Czechoslovakia has no wheels but the foreparts (protomes) of a pair of draught oxen. And from the South Polish Funnel-Beaker culture site of Bronocice is a pottery cup, again of about 3500–3000 BC with incised decoration including schematic plan views of four-wheeled wagons with draught-poles and yokes. The decoration forms a horizontal composition in which the wagons are flanked by vertical lines with oblique fringes between chequer-board panels, below which are double zigzag lines. It is perhaps not fanciful to see this as a pictorial frieze where the wagons are set between trees and areas of small ploughed fields, with water or a stream below. If so it might be compared with the undoubtedly pictorial scene on a well-known third-millennium silver bowl from Maikop in the northwest Caucasus, with mountains from which run two streams to a pool or lake, and an animal frieze of wild bull, horse, lions, boar and wild sheep. Pictorial influence from the ancient Near East has been claimed for Maikop, and perhaps it need not be excluded for Bronocice. But however we interpret this depiction, the making of fine pottery cups with wagon representations, or in the form of wagons themselves, must indicate that the vehicle has acquired a status in the contemporary world-picture of more than one Neolithic social group in middle Europe in the fourth millennium BC which transcended that of an adjunct to the farmyard. By about 2000 BC pottery models of two- and four-wheeled vehicles are frequent in ancient Mesopotamia, which may be in some sense votive or no more than toys, though the more than a dozen large copper models of ox-wagons from looted sites in Anatolia, broadly later third millennium BC, must represent prestige vehicles, and have themselves the status of tomb or votive offerings.[12] And the case is strengthened by the last and most important factor, now to be considered, the ox-drawn vehicle in funeral ritual.

The wagon burials

In a number of instances over the same area and range of time as the pottery just discussed, graves have been excavated which, together with the human interments, have burials of paired oxen, on occasion in such positions as to imply that they had been accompanied in the grave by wheeled vehicles vanished beyond trace of recognition by the excavators. In Hungary, in the same cemetery at Budakalász that produced the wagon-cup, a large grave 3.5 m long had the burials of a pair of oxen at one end, and that of a man and a woman at the other, with plenty of room for a vanished wooden vehicle. Similar circumstances obtained in at least two contemporary graves in Poland and another in Germany. We shall see in the next chapter exactly the same phenomena in Mesopotamian graves with paired equid burials in a slightly later context.

Further east, over the great area of steppe from north-east Bulgaria to the Volga, vehicle burials have been excavated in soil conditions which have enabled the recovery of whole wagons or of wheels, as well as pottery models of carts, though never of the draught animals, which were not included in the burial. These burials belong to a consistent culture and date from about 3000 to 2500 BC. These are the earliest vehicle burials in prehistory, a type which becomes a recurrent feature of the archaeology of the Old World from those of the late fourth millennium BC in South Russia, to those of Ur, Kish or Susa in the middle third; the horse-drawn chariot burials of China at the end of the second onwards, or those of the Yorkshire Wolds of the last centuries BC. In all, the locally current vehicle of prestige plays its part as a symbol of the status of the deceased, as an ostentatious demonstration of dispensable wealth at the funeral and also, if the belief-system sanctioned it, an appropriate means of transport to the otherworld and an affirmation of social standing on arrival there. The circumstances of vehicles buried in high-ranking graves throughout prehistory raise unresolved problems of function: are they to be seen as expensive status-symbols buried with the dead as a demonstration of rank and power here and beyond the grave, or are they vehicles hallowed by their funerary function of transporting the corpse to its final resting-place? Such magic functions may well be merged and interwoven, and we should recognize the fluidity of belief and practice in burial rites and not necessarily find ourselves besieged by frequent hearses.

A potentially superb series of wagon burials exists in the graves

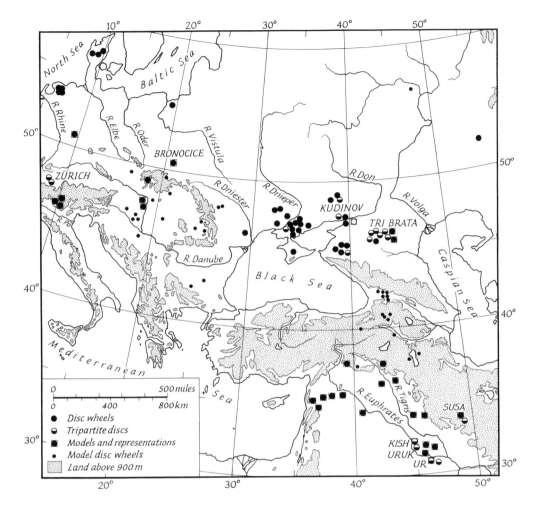

2 *Map of the evidence for wheeled vehicles before 2000 BC.*

of the South Russian Pit Graves and Catacomb Graves of the late fourth and early third millennia BC, from eastern Bulgaria to the river Volga 2000 km to the east, its southern boundary the north coast of the Black Sea. In graves under barrows (*kurgans*) something like 100 vehicle burials must have been excavated over the past forty years, increasingly in the last decades, but of these only about half have even the briefest published record, and the few fuller excavation reports that have appeared demonstrate the deplorable state of archaeology in the Soviet Union up to the present. In the field, excavation techniques are those outmoded a century ago in the West; the publications, national and provincial, are (like Browning's scrofulous French novel) printed 'on grey paper with blunt type'. A sympathetic reviewer of my 1983 attempt to interpret these records referred to their 'impenetrable awfulness'; the woeful little scratchy plans and sections (where these exist), the muddy half-tones of bad photographs, the lack of any scale drawings or technical details of the vehicle remains, constitute a melancholy memorial to ignorance or disregard of the minimal standards of international scholarship.

This is not an exercise in academic rancour but a necessary criticism of sources and a warning that we have to deal with fascinating evidence clumsily recovered and inadequately presented; that we have in fact to make the best of a pretty bad job. To summarize as best we can, the ceremonial representation of prestige vehicles in these graves took three forms: actual vehicles (all wagons); detached wheels as a *pars pro toto* representation including single pairs implying carts; and pottery models, three of carts and one of a wagon. Burials of the draught animals were not made, unlike the presumptive vehicle burials in central Europe just described, though animal offerings are frequent in the form of hide burials represented by the skulls and lower limb bones of sacrificed cattle or more frequently sheep. Such 'head and hoofs' offerings were to be increasingly frequent with the domesticated horse among the steppe peoples, surviving as a part of their underlying shamanism into this century. In the mid-third-millennium Royal Tombs at Alaca Hüyük in Anatolia, hide burials of oxen in pairs strongly suggest the representation of paired draught even though no trace of vehicles remains: these tombs are culturally linked to the copper wagon models already referred to.[13]

To return to the Pit Grave wagon burials, the available published records give something over sixteen examples of complete four-wheeled wagons (or at least wheel-and-axle units and floorboards), and in ten the remains of an arched tilt. This form of 'covered wagon' is also represented by one Pit Grave pottery model and several from the Near East of slightly later date,[14] and as we shall see, in the Pit Grave derivatives in the Caucasus of the early and middle second millennium, by complete surviving vehicles. Overall wagon lengths average around 2.0 and 2.5 m, and the distance between the wheels (the track or gauge) a remarkably consistent average of about 1.45 m. The wheels (sometimes found also in pairs as symbols of vehicles) are, as recorded, in about equal numbers simple and tripartite discs, and range in diameter from 25 cm in one detached pair, presumably from a cart, to around 70–80 cm on the wagons. All freely rotated on their fixed axles, thus enabling them to be detached when buried alone. The draught-pole of a wagon must have a flexible junction with the body to allow of some vertical movement while maintaining the vehicle with all four wheels firmly on the ground (a cart can tilt). It can therefore be detached before burial to reduce the size of the grave-pit containing the wagon, but also seems to have been present in a couple of instances as two finds of yokes are mentioned. One wagon had white-painted wheels and another was described as having back panels with incised decoration of spirals, triangles and rectangles. In the Caucasian wagons shortly to be described panels of elaborate carved woodwork survived. The covering of the arched tilts may be assumed to have been patterned matting, cloth or felt (a sheet of patterned fabric survived at the edge of the Tri Brata grave) and in all the use of colour must be envisaged, in the manner of the fifth-century BC tombs of Pazyryk in the Altai. The pottery models from the Pit Graves show arched tilts were in use on two-wheeled carts, but no examples of the actual carts have survived.

All in all, the evidence, imperfect though it is, demonstrates that in the Pit Grave burials just reviewed, we are dealing with funeral rites of a society with an hierarchical structure which permits members of an élite to demonstrate their status by burials differentiated from others by the possession of a prestige vehicle, and that alone: the other unimpressive grave-offerings are uniform in all burials, and there is no indication of social differentiation into 'rich' and 'poor' graves. One aspect of this society is attested, and that an arresting one. Reports on the human remains from the wagon-graves are few and brief, but in three instances a man and a woman are buried together (at Lola on the Kalmyk Steppe side-by-side in the wagon), and in five the burial was that of a woman alone (including

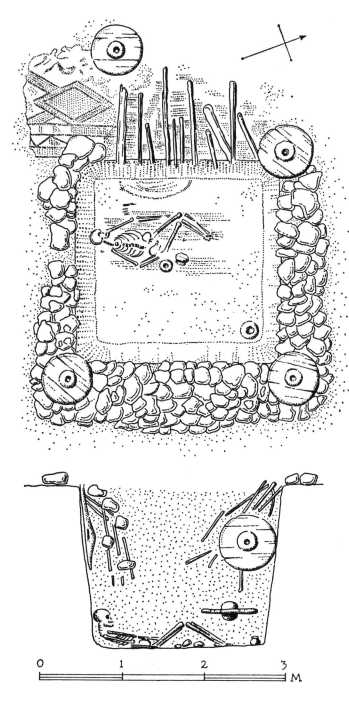

*3 Burial with tripartite disc wheels,
Tri Brata, Elista, Kalmyk ASSR.*

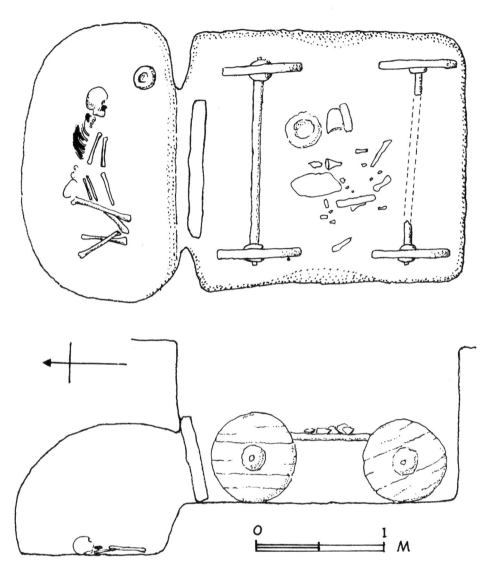

4 *Wagon burial, Elista, Kalmyk ASSR.*

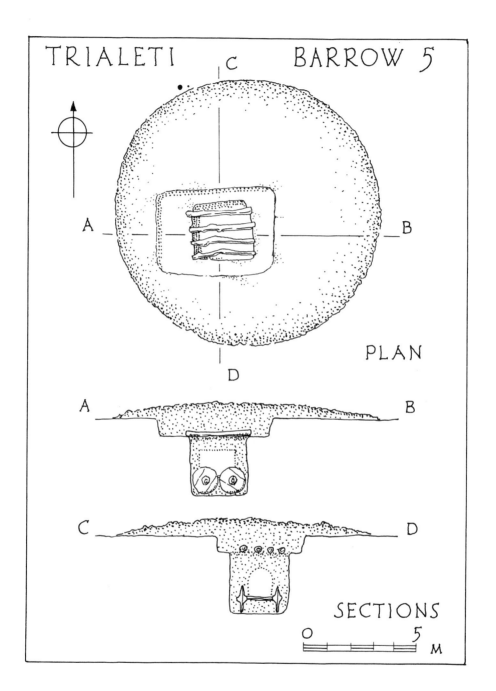

TRIALETI C BARROW 5

PLAN

A B

C D

SECTIONS

0 5
M

5 Wagon burial, Trialeti, Georgia.

the wheel-burial in Bulgaria). Privilege was clearly not confined to men within the wagon-driving aristocracy.

The last expression of this wagon-burial tradition is found in the late derivatives of the Pit Graves in the Caucasus, the tombs of Trialeti in Georgia and at Lchashen on Lake Sevan in Armenia, the former early and the latter in the middle of the second millennium BC.[15] Here again we are faced with inadequate record and publication: Kuftin's work at Trialeti was a rescue operation in 1936–40 in advance of flooding by a hydro-electric scheme, followed by the War and the excavator's death; at Lake Sevan the excavation of the cairn-covered pit tombs revealed by the reverse process (with the flood-plain around the lake, hitherto submerged, drained by another project), and carried out in 1956–58, has never seen publication beyond short interim reports. Two wagons found at Trialeti, one originally with an arched tilt, survive, of almost identical size and proportions; at Lchashen five wagons, four with arched tilts and one with wickerwork panel sides, survive, as well as five open carts and two chariots. The carts are of the triangular 'A' plan of ox-carts in the Caucasus and Sardinia until early this century, and in Anatolia today. Some tombs contained several vehicles: Barrow 2 had a covered wagon, two carts and a toy model cart accompanying the burials of twelve persons, one a child.

But at Lchashen the change of fashion which was to eclipse the prestige of the fine ox-carriage is already in evidence. Hide-burials include not only those of cattle, but of horses; in two graves there are not only the heavy disc-wheeled wagons but light spoked-wheeled chariots, and bronze models of horse-drawn chariots also occur. The horse, already established in prestige in the ancient Near Eastern civilizations by early in the second millennium BC, was beginning its take-over and its rise in the social scale, adding to the range of conspicuous ostentation another vanity, that of speed. That the ox-wagon maintained some higher esteem than a farm adjunct is suggested by the fine pottery models of disc-wheeled wagons among the Bronze Age communities within the Carpathian Ring of about 2500–1700 BC. But contemporary models of spoked wheels, and elements of horse harness such as the cheek-pieces of bits, in the same area, point the way to the impending change following the adoption of the light, horse-drawn, two-wheeled vehicle ancestral to the chariot.[16]

The ox-wagon in decline

In the later prehistory of ox-draught in Eurasia, carts and wagons alike slide into the obscurity of archaeology, and when they re-emerge in iconography or, in a world of increasing literacy, in texts, they no longer have pretentions to grandeur, but are obscurely utilitarian among the lower ranks of society. In the reliefs of Medinet Habu commemorating the victory of Ramesses III over the invading 'Sea Peoples' in 1186 BC, the enemy have, as well as horse-drawn chariots, ox carts with disc wheels (and with linch pins and so rotating on fixed axles), and one with openwork sides.[17]

In Greece, the earliest evidence for ox draught is textual, and contained in the Linear B tablets of 1400–1200 BC in Mycenaean Greece. Here the palace scribes are concerned with 'working' oxen which could draw ploughs or carts (not themselves specified), but one unexpected detail appears to liven the bureaucratic aridity of the records, half a dozen of the nicknames of individual beasts.[18] Through their classic Greek forms they can be rendered colloquially as Blacky, Chestnut and Winey (red), Speedy and Bellower, and Lightfoot or Whitefoot, a name (*podargos*) shared by a chariot-horse in the Iliad.[19] The names take us from the oxen on the plain of Argos across the centuries and a continent to Jean Ingelow's cows in a Victorian English meadow

> Come uppe Whitefoot, come uppe Lightfoot,
> Come uppe Jetty, rise and follow,
> Jetty, to the milking shed.[20]

The affectionate naming of domestic animals was powerful and symbolic in rural societies. The name took the animal literally from the herd and recognized it as an individual, and at the same time incorporated it as a no longer anonymous member of the bucolic family and household: parents and children, the huntsman's or shepherd's dog, the mousing cat, the beasts in stall and stable, each united within a group linked by verbal bonds.[21]

In general, ancient Greece, from Homer and Hesiod in the eighth century BC, distinguished between two main types of vehicle, the two-wheeled chariot, *harma*, invariably horse-drawn, and the wagon or carriage, four-wheeled and drawn usually by mules or asses, less often oxen, *amaxa*.[22] Prestige spoked-wheeled carriages, like Priam's splendid vehicle, are drawn by mules (*Iliad* XXIV, 265–274), but some of the wagons carrying logs for Hector's funeral pyre at the

6 Cart of the Sea Peoples shown on an Egyptian relief of c.1186 BC.

end of the epic (XXIV, 782) are pulled by oxen; in the *Odyssey* (6) Nausicaa drives the mules of an *amaxa* (with the palace laundry and a picnic lunch) to the washing-place on the river bank. In Hesiod's Tasks for the Year – the *Works and Days* – we are in the world of the peasant farmer with a single pair of draught oxen for plough or wagon as need arises. His elliptical directions for making a wheels-and-axle unit seem to indicate a spoked or more likely a composite 'cross-bar' wheel, an actual example of which, of the early fifth century BC, was found at Olympia, and which are frequent on light country carts in vase paintings of around the same date, all drawn by equids.[23]

One ox-wagon in antiquity rose in the world to achieve fame and sanctity, that at the Phrygian capital of Gordion in Anatolia. Arrian, writing in the second century AD his life of Alexander (*Anabasis* II, 3), tells the legend of how 'in the ancient days' a poor Phrygian farmer named Gordius had two ox-teams, one for his plough and one for his wagon. Omens started with an eagle perching on the plough-team; then the Phrygian oracle announced that 'a wagon will bring them a king'. Gordius, his wife and children, including his son Midas, drove in their ox-wagon into the local town soon after and the oracle was fulfilled: Midas was made king and the wagon was preserved as a sacred relic, with a prophecy that whoever loosened the 'cunningly tied cord of cornel bark' holding the yoke to the draught pole would be Lord of Asia. Alexander visited Gordion in 333 BC and found the wagon in what was known as the Palace of Gordius and Midas: the city dates from the eighth century BC as the Phrygian capital and a Midas (perhaps a title) was an historical king of Phrygia 738–696 BC. Whether Alexander actually 'cut the Gordian knot' or pulled out the belaying-pin round which it was lashed at the pole end is a matter of uncertain mythology. Yoke lashings were well known to be complicated affairs, and that of Priam's mule-carriage just mentioned takes seven lines of sonorous Homeric hexameters to describe.

The Roman world shared the technological inertia of that of Greece. Latin has a rich vocabulary of vehicle-names, many of which are loan-words from Celtic: Cisalpine and Transalpine Gaul shared an inventiveness in transport technology which was to contribute to the post-classical alertness in innovations of early medieval Europe.[24] The Roman ox, as in Greece, was typically the beast of the plough and secondarily of transport, where mules and asses served for most purposes of traction and pack-carrying. These too could also draw the heavy-duty cart particularly associated with ox-draught, the *plaustrum.*[25] Varro, Cato and Virgil describe it as a part of a farm's equipment, but it does not figure in the agronomists Columella and Palladius. It normally was a two-wheeled cart, though Cato's *plaustra maiora* are taken to be four-wheelers, like the other Celtic types, the *raeda* and the *petorritum*; by the seventh century Isidore of Seville firmly wrote *plaustrum vehiculum duarum rotarum.* An anonymous scholiast, once thought to be the second-century Probus, wrote of Virgil's mention of *plaustra* in Georgics I, 163 'Plaustra are vehicles of which the wheels are not spoked but drums [i.e. discs] fixed to the axle and bound with an iron tyre. The axle therefore turns with the wheel.' Small wonder that they screeched (*stridentia plaustra*). Anyone who has been at dusk in a village on the Anatolian plateau will recall the distant squealing of the ox-carts, similarly disc-wheeled with fixed axles, returning from the fields: I was told that each housewife, recognizing the individual note of her husband's cart from afar, took it as the signal to put on the supper.

And so the humble ox-cart creaks and groans its way into bucolic oblivion, save for one remarkable appearance as a vehicle of high prestige in early medieval Europe. Before leaving the Roman world and turning to the Europe which followed the break-up of the Empire we should remember one general point. The interpretation of vehicle technology over this period is by no means easy despite an abundance of sources, lexical and literary on the one hand and iconographic and pictorial on the other, for in no instance can the two be directly linked. We have just discussed *plaustrum* in the texts: there are several representations of two-wheeled carts in Roman sculpture and mosaics but we can only assume that these would be called *plaustra* by Latin speakers. So too with the rest of the extensive vocabulary – *raeda* and *petorritum, covinnus* and *essedum* (and as we shall particularly see, *carpentum*) – convincing matching of text to image can be no more than an assumption or a complete guess. This has not inhibited past scholars from presenting these as facts, as the works of reference almost up to today show, full of convincing pictures of named vehicles. Much blame must be attached to the German master coach-builder J.C. Ginzrot, who in 1817 published a detrimentally influential treatise on classical vehicles, full of illustrations of confident identifications or of the sheer inventions of an all too clever modern craftsman. So seductive were Ginzrot's pictures that they were copied again and again in the dictionaries of classical antiquities to obtain a spurious validity up to the present.[26]

The ox-cart of the kings

By the fifth century AD the Roman Empire was crumbling, but Christian. Beyond its shrunken frontiers in what had been Roman Gaul there lay the territories of the pagan barbarians of the north, notably the Franks. Here the Merovingian dynastic line was established by the shadowy Merovech, on whose death in AD 456 his son Childeric I came to the throne; he died in 481 as the most famous of the pagan line. Childeric's son, Clovis I, was converted to Christianity soon after 493 and died in 511, to be followed by an increasingly inefficient succession of Christian Merovingian kings under whom power slipped more and more into the hands of the mayors of the palace until in 754 the last king, Childeric III, was deposed and the mayor of the day, Pepin the Short, was crowned King of the Franks by Pope Stephen III. In the new dynasty Charles, *Carolus magnus*, Charlemagne, became king in 768 and, establishing himself as the outstanding warrior and statesman of Europe, was crowned Holy Roman Emperor by Pope Leo III on Christmas Day 800, reigning until his death in 814.

This historical resumé is necessary to understand the story of prestige transport and the demeanour of monarchs in motion in early medieval Europe. As we shall see in later chapters, the ox-wagon as a status symbol for the top levels of society was to be overtaken by equid draught, notably the horse-drawn chariot, from early in the second millennium BC. Thereafter the prestige chariot for display and warfare was to dominate a whole series of disparate societies in Greece, Egypt, the Levant and Mesopotamia, India and China for centuries until the break-up of much of the western civilized world – until around 1000 BC, when already the alternative prestige of the ridden horse, of the cavalryman rather than the charioteer, was beginning to be apparent. In the west, by the time of the classical world of Greece and Rome, chariotry had become a survival in contexts of symbolic parade, religious ceremonial and racing (itself originally part of religious observance), to be replaced on formal and state occasions by horsemanship. In early medieval Europe the northern Germanic pagans were riders much concerned, as were their eastern neighbours the nomads of the Eurasian steppes, with sacred horses, rituals, sacrifices and burials: we shall come later to the horse-sacrifices round the tomb of Childeric I. With the rise of the Carolingian dynasty, its members saw their destiny as leaders of a *renovatio* of the classical past and consciously turned for models to the great men of a dimly apprehended past glory, the Roman Empire whose rulers, like themselves, made their formal appearance on horseback. Charlemagne, as Emperor of the new Holy Roman Empire, consciously pursued this emulation of *romanitas*, and, a fine horseman, saw himself as *imperator*, the embodiment of the ancient and heroic equestrian monarch. It was therefore with somewhat pained surprise that his biographer Einhard found himself bound to chronicle that the last Merovingian kings made their ceremonial appearance in ox-carts.[27]

Einhard was an able and learned cleric who for over twenty years served as a member of Charlemagne's court and after his monarch's death wrote, between 829 and 856, his life. In the opening paragraph he describes how Childeric III, the last of the Merovingian line,

content with his royal title, he would sit on the throne, with his hair long and his beard flowing, and act the part of a ruler ... Whenever he needed to travel, he went in a cart which was drawn in country style by yoked oxen, with a cowherd to drive them. In this fashion he would go to the palace and to the general assembly of his people ... and in this fashion he would return again.

For Einhard the moral was clear. The degenerate later Merovingians, those effeminate *rois fénéants* with their unkempt hair, finally demeaned themselves by the slovenly rusticity of their state transport, whereas the new king was a real man who sat proudly on his steed like a Roman Emperor, *dux et imperator* of his people. Many modern historians seem to have taken Einhard's point of view. Louis Halphen, editing the Latin text of the *Vita Caroli* in 1923, referred regretfully to 'the fanciful tone of this page, which has for too long distorted the history of the eighth century'; Wallace-Hadrill in 1952 wrote of the last Merovingian kings that 'they remained at home, taking we know not what part in the life of their people, pottering round their estates on their ox-wagons'. Lewis Thorpe, however, editing his translation of Einhard in 1969, saw it differently: 'the cart ... like the long hair and beards of the Merovingian kings, was really a sign of their royal and religious dignity'.[28] Since no one seems to have reconsidered the subject in the light of the modern knowledge of archaeology and vehicle technology set out earlier in this chapter, it may be apposite to do so now.

To begin with we now see how the ox, the first domestic animal to draw wheeled transport, achieved appropriate prestige, with its cart or wagon, to serve the upper levels of societies by 3000 BC by being a status symbol fit to accompany some members of these social groups to the grave. It would be over a millennium before the horse in its arrogance came to take over, first for draught and later, by classical times, as the ridden animal which alone was held appropriate for the leaders of the state. In the Roman world, and that which came after in western Europe, the ethos had been fixed firmly enough: a gentleman and above all one who wished to command, and demonstrate command over other men, must ride a horse; the ruler as a cavalry general. Slow-moving wheeled vehicles such as ceremonial chariots or carriages might carry appropriate persons in triumphs, pageants and rituals, but there was a tradition established that closed carriages were suitable only to the ladies of the court, or to priests.

If we now turn to the text of Einhard's *Vita* we immediately run up against the problem already touched on, the uncertainty of Latin vehicle-names. In the passage just quoted Einhard uses the term *carpentum: Quocumque eundum erat, carpento ibat, quod bubus juncti et bubulco rustico more agente trahebatur.* Now he was a careful Latin stylist, and modelled his Charlemagne biography on those of the *De vita Caesarum* of the second-century author Suetonius, especially that of Augustus. His use of *carpentum*, a term used by Suetonius more than once,[29] may therefore be derived from his classical model and need not reflect ninth-century usage.

Carpentum is a tricky word which I discussed in 1983.[30] It is Celtic in origin, contained in place-names such as the Gaulish *Carpentorate* (Carpentras) or the lost *Carbantoritum* in North Britain, and is ancestral to the Old Irish *carpat*, a chariot or light two-wheeled cart (and indeed ultimately to modern English 'carpenter'). In classical Latin it is used by, for instance, Livy and Florus for Gaulish war-chariots, but its general familiar usage (as in Suetonius) was for a covered civil vehicle used especially for women and on priestly occasions in the Roman world, and usually drawn by mules or asses, not horses. It became a general word for a two-wheeler and by the fourth century could be used for a dung-cart. The encyclopaedist Isidore Bishop of Seville in the seventh century knew of *carpentum pompaticum vehiculi genus, quasi carrum pompaticum,*[31] and vehicles which would fit this appellation, with an elaborately ornamented arched tilt, are shown on reliefs and coins, like that struck by the Emperor Gaius to commemorate his mother Agrippina on his accession in AD 37.[32] It seems reasonable therefore that in using *carpentum* of the ox-drawn carriage of Childeric III, Einhard not only used Suetonian phraseology, but one carrying with it overtones of effeminacy as well as display.

This leads to a final point. The ceremonial wearing of long hair by the Frankish kings was a matter of comment from the time of Claudian about AD 400; the intaglio portrait on the gold signet ring of Childeric I, put in his grave in 481, shows him with shoulder-length locks.[33] Marc Bloch noted the magic element in this as a part of international folklore of which Samson is one figure out of many. He also made reference to suggestions by Chadwick and others that the ceremonial ox-cart of the Merovingians might be related to the passage in Tacitus (*Germ.* XL) describing the procession of the Nordic goddess Nerthus in a sacred carriage drawn by heifers – 'perhaps a seductive hypothesis, but in the long run no more than that'.[34] Let us momentarily be seduced. The Franks had come south from the archaeological areas of what I have called 'Cimbric Wagons', ceremonial four-wheeled carriages known from votive bog-finds as at Djebjerg or in graves such as Husby: the Nerthus vehicle is wholly appropriate here.[35] Perhaps we should think again of this Nordic tradition and even of the hint of androgynous links between Nerthus, the lank-haired goddess figures shown on the cauldrons of Gundestrup or Rynkeby, and the long-haired Frankish kings in their sacerdotal aspect. Perhaps Einhard was more right than he knew when he chose *carpentum*.

Epilogue: Ox-carts and British Rail

As we saw earlier on, the wheel-tracks or gauge of prehistoric ox-carts, from that at Zürich of the early third millennium BC to those at Lchashen of a millennium and a half later, had maintained a remarkably consistent width of between 1.30 and 1.60 m in the recorded examples, averaging 1.45 m. To anticipate, this was maintained in prehistoric Europe with horse-drawn carriages and chariots, *c.*600–100 BC, averaging 1.30 m; Roman cart-ruts average 1.40 m. As this must have meant adherence to a round number of units, five 'short feet' of about 11.40 inches would fit, and such short foot units were common in antiquity, and up until modern standardized measurements were imposed by legislation. At the end of the last century English farm wagons had considerable regional variants, their extremes somewhere between 1.30 m and 1.90 m. About 40 years ago an old gentleman told me that when he moved from the West Country on inheriting his present Lincolnshire estate in the 1880s he had to have all his farmyard and personal vehicles altered 'to fit the Lincolnshire ruts – like tramlines'. He would indeed, by about 10 in between south-west and north-east. In Yorkshire the Dales wagon of the last century had a gauge of 4 ft 4 in, the Moor wagon 5 ft.[36] When George Stephenson came to build his Stockton to Darlington railway line in 1825 he built it to a local gauge of 4 ft 8 in, and this, modified by a half inch to 4 ft 8½ in by Act of Parliament in 1828 when the line was extended from Stockton to Middlesborough, was made compulsory in 1846.[37] This has remained standard for British railway lines until the present day – 1.43 m as compared with the prehistoric average of 1.45 m for ox-wagons from Switzerland to the Caucasus, and for railways on the Continent from 1832. British Rail has inherited a strangely ancient legacy.

II
Chariots and Chariotry

We saw in the last chapter that by around 3000–2500 BC the ox-drawn wagon or carriage had achieved the status of a prestige vehicle, worthy of being given ceremonial burial with its owner, in central and southeastern Europe from the Carpathians to the Volga, and again in Mesopotamia. Technically the vehicles shared the feature of simple or composite disc wheels, normally tripartite, rendering difficult any estimate of priority of invention between east and west in this extensive area. If the concept of innovating as against conserving societies is thought to have a validity, descriptive of situations even while not explaining their origins, clearly the invention and adoption of wheeled vehicles took place among innovating societies over this large and varied terrain. One outstanding society within the larger group is that centred in ancient Mesopotamia which, owing to its early development of another technical innovation, that of writing, enables us to see it as successively peopled by speakers of the Sumerian language (of unknown or very uncertain affiliations), and of a member of the Semitic linguistic family, Akkadian, in the Babylonian and Assyrian kingdoms. We therefore have ancient literate civilizations rather than communities with simpler social systems with a more restricted technology to deal with, and so to the purely archaeological evidence of material culture we can, to our immense advantage, add written texts.

So far as wheeled transport goes, the ancient Sumerians shared with those other peoples, from Neolithic Europe on the west to the bronze-using civilization of the Indus Valley to the east, the use of the ox-drawn wagon or cart from the beginning of the third millennium BC. That ox-wagons could, as on the South Russian steppe, play a symbolic rôle in the burials of an upper stratum of society, reflecting their prestige as carriages for the living, is shown by the remains of disc-wheeled wagons and bovid skeletons in princely tombs of Early Dynastic III date, *c.*2500 BC, in the Ur Royal Cemetery (Grave PG 580: four bovids and a probable vehicle; PG 789: 6 bovids and two four-wheelers; bovids uncertainly with Puabi's throne sledge in PG 800) and again at Kish and Susa less well recorded.[1] But inventiveness was in the air, and experiments with alternative draught animals were already being made, exploring the potentialities of a different group of wild animals, the equids. To these we must now turn.

Equids in Mesopotamia: ass, onager and horse

We begin with basic zoology. The mammalian genus *Equus* is divided into six distinct sub-genera or species: *E. asinus* the wild ass and domestic donkey, *E. hemionus* the 'half ass' or onager, and *E. ferus*, probably divisible into two sub-species, *E. ferus przewalskii*, Przewalsky's horse and *E. ferus gmelni*, the Tarpan. The remaining three species of *Equus* are the zebras, *hippotigris*, *quagga* and *dolichohippus*, which are confined to continental Africa and so do not concern us in Asia and Europe. It appears that zoologists are not themselves unanimous in their taxonomy of *Equus* and as late as the 1960s could indulge in what the more sceptical Colin Groves recently called 'making horses out of thin air' (for instance one scheme has 18 horses, 4 hemiones and 4 'others').[2] The confusion inherent here has been worse confounded by those enthusiastic horse-lovers who, their hippophile hearts running away with their unscientific heads, have uncritically indulged in breeds and strains, hot blood and cold blood, Arabs and Thoroughbreds and the rest, to obscure rather than clarify varieties of *Equus caballus*. This, the domesticated horse descended from *E. ferus* and distinguished from it by having the chromosome number 64 as against the 66 of the surviving Przewalsky's horse, has, as we shall see, distinctive 'groups' (rather than 'types' or 'breeds') but is otherwise a unitary sub-species. So far as the chromosome relationship goes, *asinus* has the number of 62, *hemionus* 56.[3]

Crucial to our present enquiry is the natural habitat of the critical three wild species at the time of their potential exploitation by man in the late fourth millennium BC, for all were involved. The wild ass, *E. asinus (africanus)* was until recent years regarded by zoologists as restricted to Africa (Nubia, Somalia) with its first domestication in Egypt, from the early third millennium, from Nubian stock. More recently a case has been put up for extending its wild habitat eastwards, from Palestine to the upper Euphrates and Tigris and the western Zagros foothills. This would overlap with *E. hemionus*, the onager, which had until recently a wide distribution from Syria to Turkmenia and even an Indian variety in the Rann of Kutch, but the two species could co-exist, the ass preferring stony broken country or low hills, the onager the flat desert. Finally, and in the long run the most important, was the horse, *E. ferus*, a species of temperate latitudes known from South Russia to Mongolia, and south of the Black Sea from Transcaucasia in suitable plateau grasslands westwards to the steppe around Eskişehir in western Anatolia.[4]

We shall return to the horse later in more detail, but for the present the important point to emerge from the zoology, archaeology and textual evidence from third-millennium Mesopotamia in recent years is that the first experiments in equid draught for prestige vehicles were made using donkeys and various suspected hybrid crosses with onagers at first and later horses. The species will interbreed, but produce only sterile offspring, the mule (*E. asinus* ♂ × *E. cabullus* ♀) being the best known and most important, from antiquity to today. Zeuner's claim of 1963[5] for domesticated onagers, which for long held the field, seems now inadmissible by most zoologists. In what follows it will be convenient to use the term 'donkey' for the domestic animal, reserving 'ass' for zoological taxonomy (and the early modern literary usage, as in the Authorized Version of the Bible).

Evidence for experimentation with draught animals other than oxen comes from graves, depictions in art, and from Sumerian (and later, Akkadian) cuneiform texts. In the Early Dynastic III Royal Cemetery at Ur, as we saw, disc-wheeled vehicles were buried with their draught oxen; in PG 1232 were wheels and a pair of donkeys. In slightly earlier (ED II) tombs at Kish, in Grave II was a four-wheeled carriage and four donkeys, in III remains of three similar vehicles and another pair; at Lagash an ED IIIB burial of a human and an equid either a donkey or an onager. In graves recently excavated at Abu Salabikh between Nippur and Babylon no. 162 had four donkeys, buried in two pairs as if in harnessed teams. Again in the Hamrin Basin northeast of Baghdad, in Tell Razuk Grave 12 a similar pair lay in a position which definitely precludes an accompanying vehicle but in another tomb of *c.*2300 BC, a donkey pair was separated by some 2.5 m from the human skeleton by a space clear of pottery or other grave-goods in exactly the manner of the paired ox-burials with suspected vanished vehicles in Neolithic Central Europe of somewhat earlier date, already referred to in the last chapter. In Mesopotamia, donkey burials go on from this their initial date of rather before 2500 BC to contexts of the Third Dynasty of Ur (*c*.2100) and Old Babylonian (*c*.1700 BC). In all, the animals are *E. asinus*, with possible cross-breeding with *E. hemionus* or even conceivably *E. caballus*.[6] Zoologists are divided about the status of the onager – wholly wild (it was certainly hunted in later Assyrian times), tamed for interbreeding or wholly domesticated – but there is something of a consensus that the third-millennium draught equids were basically donkeys and certainly not horses. Mary Littauer and Joost Crouwel some years ago wrote of the artistic representations of equids drawing vehicles at this period that they seem 'seldom if ever horses' and that it is 'impossible to tell whether domestic ass, tamed native hemione or any other possible crosses were favoured'.[7]

Even if the representations of wheeled vehicles in Mesopotamia from *c*.2500 BC may fail us in respect of the zoological details of the draught equids involved, the types of vehicles they drew is clearly depicted. In general, on the reliefs and inlays of the period, and the beautiful cire-perdue copper model from Tell Agrab, we see heavy four- or two-wheeled conveyances with disc or tripartite solid wheels, sometimes with the tread armoured with metal stud-nails, and drawn by teams of two or four beasts. I went into the technology some years ago and here will merely say that I distinguished (in engineering terms) the heavy compression-structures with disc wheels from those, from the second millennium BC onwards, which were tension-structures of light bent wood with spoked wheels, and called the first 'battle cars' while reserving the term 'chariot' for the latter. I would now prefer, for reasons shortly to be discussed, to drop the exclusively warlike connotation of 'battle' in favour of 'parade' cars, while emphasizing that the lightly built chariot brought with it the potentialities of greater speed as a new enhancement of prestige in transport both in peace and war. What the various representations from the third millennium BC onwards make clear is that the yoke-harnessing of paired bovid draught was continued with that of equids, though anatomically inappropriate. This well-known conservatism, though less constrictive for horses than Lefebvre des Noettes first claimed in his classic study of 1931,[8] nevertheless became an obstructive archaism until the first experiments of harnessing between shafts were made in Imperial Roman times in the west and in second-century AD China, followed by its combination with the rigid collar from the fifth century, and in western Europe from around the ninth century, as we shall see in a later chapter.

The cuneiform texts may be briefly referred to here. The Sumerian, from the end of the third millennium BC, show the use of a generic 'equid' word, *anse* covering asses and their hybrids, onagers and horses, distinguished by qualifying epithets in which for instance 'equid of the desert' denoted an ass or donkey, and 'equid of the mountain' meaning a horse, reaching the Mesopotamian plain from the mountainous north. Since henceforward we are concerned with the horse as the uniquely prestigious traction animal, we must for the time being leave the donkeys and mules of antiquity, to return to them later in the context of the riders of princely steeds. A further technological aspect contained in the Sumerian and Akkadian texts is the nomenclature of the vehicle which, starting as a heavy parade car, became the chariot of the ancient Near East and beyond. Sumerian seems to have had two main vehicle words, one *mar-gid-da* for a four-wheeled draught wagon (*eriqqu* in Akkadian), and the other *gigir*, a general all-purpose vehicle word but especially for one with two wheels, the cuneiform character for which shows a stylized disc wheel. In Akkadian this was equated with another all-purpose word from a Semitic 'conveyance' root, *narkabtu*, which then became specialized as a chariot, invariably horse-drawn, whereas the Akkadian heavy-duty wagon, *sumbu*, was drawn by mules or, as traditionally, oxen.[9] With *narkabtu* then, we come to the beginning of one of the great chapters of ancient history; the development of the light two-wheeled chariot drawn by paired horses as a piece of technology and as an institution within the social order as an emblem of power and prestige. Chariotry was to play its part, in some form or another, not only in the ancient Near Eastern Akkadian world from soon after 2000 BC, but soon in Egypt, in the Hittite world and the Caucasus; Mycenaean Greece follows, then India, China and the Levant; barbarian northwest Europe and the Mediterranean and North Africa westwards to Spain by the seventh century BC, in Britain finally by the second century BC. As a widespread symbol of élite transport for monarch and nobles the chariot, and the mystique of chariotry, was to lose its prestige in favour of the ridden steed by the first millennium BC, but throughout the previous thousand years it had embodied for much of the known world monarchy in motion.

Chariots and chariotry: the basic requirements

Here we enter, or at least nervously cross the frontiers of, a world of archaeological and historical discussion which has generated a library of commentary and exegesis over decades of devoted and often controversial scholarship.[10] For our purpose we must consider it as an episode in the history of prestige transport and to that end I feel that an important distinction should be made at the outset which has not hitherto been given the weight it deserves, a distinction which may help to clarify a complex situation. There seem to me to be two things that should be separated which have too often been conflated and confused. The first is basically technological: the invention, development and primary use of a new vehicle which unlike the earlier ox-drawn wagon or cart took advantage of a novel tractive force, the domesticated horse, coupled with the construction of a light, strong two-wheeled car for one or two persons which would enable the horse's agility and swiftness to be exploited and achieve the hitherto unfulfilled psychological excitement of speed in motion. This combination of swift motive power and a vehicle appropriate to its employment, however used, was the chariot. There then could develop, not inevitably but only in certain social circumstances, the institutionalized and stylized use of such fast conveyances in organized form, in peace and war, and be expressed as chariotry. The application of such a distinction to the wide-ranging use of light, fast, horse-drawn conveyances in antiquity simplifies a complex state of affairs and renders it more comprehensible. Evidence for the chariot as a vehicle is not evidence for chariotry as an institution. We will start with the vehicle and then assess the demands it would have made on the individual or corporate owner; what in a world of non-monetary economies it would cost to install and maintain such a status-conferring means of transport, the price of prestige.

We may best begin within the Mesopotamian area at the beginning of the second millennium BC, where the essential chariot type can be seen from texts and depictions (largely on seals). As a piece of technology it needed raw materials not always all locally available, and above all its essential motive power, the horse. The domesticated, broken-in, trained horse was in itself as much an artifact as the chariot, but the 'equid of the mountains' was, in wild or domestic form, a foreigner from its natural habitat, in the temperate climatic zone to the north and the open pasturage of steppe or semi-steppe.

The wild ancestor of *Equus caballus*, the domestic horse with a chromosome number of 64, is represented today by the subspecies *Equus ferus przewalskii*, Przewalsky's horse, with 66 chromosomes, now surviving in zoos (but sighted wild up to the 1960s in Outer Mongolia). Zoologists are divided on the question of the Tarpan horse surviving on the Ukrainian steppe until the end of the nineteenth century: Sandor Bökönyi classes it as a sub-species, *E. ferus gmelini*, while Juliet Clutton-Brock regards it as feral and takes *przewalskii* as the only truly wild species. A geneticist, Roger Short, speculated that the Tarpan might have had 64 chromosomes.[11] We may never know, but bio-anthropological work is in progress on determining blood groups and genetic features from bones. Some form of *E. ferus* – or *E. caballus*, or both – is known over a wide geographical area to the north and south of the Black Sea from *c.*4500 to 3580 BC. Of this earliest group, archaeologically in the Sredny Stog culture between the rivers Dnieper and Don in South Russia, we have reliable modern knowledge, both archaeological and zoological, and secure radiocarbon dating. The plentiful horse bones in the settlement sites show it was basically a food animal, but there is also evidence of control for riding with bits, and ritual horse burials.[12] In subsequent prehistory the domestic horse is common to the Urals and beyond. All this is steppe country but similar terrain, though discontinuous, is available from Transcaucasia westwards and south of the Pontic Range in Anatolia, where horse remains, more probably wild than domestic, appear in the Kura-Araxes culture from Shengavit near Erevan into eastern Turkey (with dates from before 3500 BC) and in sites of comparable date around Elazig and again at the extreme west of the Anatolian steppe around Eskişehir.[13] From Maikop at the western end of the Caucasus comes a well-known silver bowl from a tomb of *c.*2500 BC with a fine naturalistic engraving of a wild horse of Przewalsky type.[14] It is this region then, around the Black Sea and from the areas to the south from Transcaucasia westward into Anatolia, that would provide a natural reservoir from which Mesopotamian horse supplies could ultimately be drawn through intermediaries who would have domesticated and trained chariot stock.

The appearance of the horse in ancient Mesopotamia comes at the point of time when equid burials die out, but texts increase around 2000 BC. One of the earliest and best-known references is in a hymn of self-praise by Shulgi, second and greatest king of the Third Dynasty of Ur, around 2100–2050 BC, where he boasts of the speed of his day's journey of 80 miles from Nippur to Ur as equal to that of a donkey, a mule, a 'horse with a waving tail' and a lion – the last metaphorical but the others presumably as transport by some means.[15] Can we say what Shulgi's horse might have been like? All early horses were within the modern pony class in withers height: Przewalsky's horse averages 135 cm (13½ hands). From the earlier seventeenth century BC we have horse burials in Egypt and Anatolia – at Buhen *c*.1675 BC, at Osmanskayasi seventeenth-sixteenth century, at Thebes 1430–1400 – with heights from 140 to 150 cm; the yoke heights of surviving Egyptian chariots average 135 cm. And we can go a stage further. When studying horse remains from central and eastern prehistoric Europe Bökönyi found he could split them into two categories for which he used the word 'groups...instead of the denominations 'type' or 'breed' since the former would refer to genetical differences and the latter to the assumption of planned stock-breeding, whereas neither appears to be proved'.[16] The Eastern group, found east of a line from approximately Venice to Vienna, includes the superior horses from the famous Pazyryk tombs in the Altai, described later on; the Western is represented by the so-called 'Celtic pony' of Exmoor type, and both are indigenous domesticates from wild Przewalsky-Tarpan stock. The Eastern group show the characteristics ancestral to the modern 'Arab' strain and formed a northwest Asiatic phenomenon. When Juliet Clutton-Brock came to examine the mid-second-millennium BC horse skeletons from Egypt and Anatolia just mentioned, she noted that they 'have all the looks of the present-day Arab breed' and that the osteological evidence was confirmed by the Egyptian Eighteenth Dynasty representations. The bone report on the horse remains from Troy VI (*c*.1800–1300 BC) described them as of 'oriental type',[17] presumably implying the same characteristics. It looks then as if the first ancient Near Eastern chariot horses included or perhaps were predominantly of Bökönyi's Eastern group.

The technological requirements of the chariot as a structure apart from its motive power are less complicated and less restricted in geographical origins. The qualities sought for were lightness and strength to meet requirements, notably speed, unattainable by the disc-wheeled wagon or cart drawn by oxen, or donkeys or mule-type hybrids, and this was obtained, as we saw, by replacing a compression with a tension structure. This was achieved by using bent wood to form, with skilled jointing techniques, glue, leather and metal, a light resilient freely moving vehicle with two spoked wheels, innovations which may owe nothing to disc wheels except their rotary function. We know the end product not only from increasingly accurate depictions, but from superb surviving examples from Egyptian tombs (including six from the tomb of Tutankhamun) *pl. 3* over the century *c.*1440–1330 BC. A few wood identifications have been made – tamarisk, elm and birch-bark – of which tamarisk is locally available, but elm and birch must have come from the temperate woodlands of north Syria and Anatolia.[18] The contemporary Mycenaean Greek documents mention elm, willow and cypress, and the very late, immediately pre-Roman, northwest European and British finds of wheels of chariot type include elm, ash, willow and hornbeam in their structure.[19] Here of course all the wood is local.

The resultant vehicle was a piece of sophisticated craftsmanship in need of watchful maintenance when in use and careful preservation over periods of inaction. Above all the light spoked wheels had to be prevented from distortion by taking the weight off the box and draught pole by removing them or supporting the whole.[20] The Mycenaean texts show dismantled wheels and bodies separately stored and inventoried,[21] and the *Iliad* has the wheels as a separate unit attached to the body before use (V, 722) and the whole vehicle when not in use leant against a wall (VIII, 435) as in the *Odyssey* (4,42), or 'set on a stand with a cloth spread over it' (VIII, 441); similar dismantling and setting on a stand is alluded to in the Vedic texts from India.[22]

The price of prestige: the chariot package-deal

So much for the basic material necessities for any individual or corporation – state, palace, temple, priesthood, army – proposing in English Victorian terms to set up a gig and become carriage folk. In our brief survey of prestige on wheels in antiquity we may now conveniently recapitulate and summarize what was needed to achieve this status and how much it cost in terms of value in non-monetary economies. Some time ago I discussed this theme in the instance of prehistoric Celtic chariots and now propose a wider review from a slightly different angle. Essentially it involved the acquisition of a techno-complex, a package-deal.[23]

In the first place the motive power was the horse, an animal with a natural habitat in the temperate climatic zones of Eurasia, and with regional variants. An adequate supply of wild or feral horses had to be available, at hand or by import through reciprocal exchange, to be available for selection and training if not for deliberate breeding of improved stock. Training for working in matched pairs could be highly organized and elaborate, as we know from extant texts, the most famous and complete being that of the Mitannian horse-trainer Kikulli in Hittite of about the fifteenth century BC.[24] Such highly trained animals needed adequate housing, foddering and watering by skilled stable staff. There is from the beginning the need for horse traders and trainers, grooms, stable lads and the like on the domestic or institutional pay-roll, and they appear in the palace archives of the eighteenth century BC at Chagar Bazar and Mari in Mesopotamia. In the early stages of chariot adoption they may be outsiders – strangers within the gates accepted as skilled technicians like the Athenian metics. Such was Kikulli, the Mitannian in Hittite service who called himself a 'horse trainer', using an Indo-Iranian title as we shall see.

So too trained constructional and maintenance staff would need to be a part of any large establishment for the building and repair of the chariots and their harness, with provision of stocks of raw materials – special seasoned woods, leather, glue and metal for structural and decorative use, paints and colourings. Here joiners and wheelwrights as well as metal-workers and artists combined their skills in creating a costly product which would need housing and storage, dismembering and re-assembling as well as emergency work after accidents which we know, from texts as far apart as India and China, were recognized hazards in the field: the Vedic texts indeed not only recognize a chariot-builder (*rathakara*) but also *rathabhresa*, a chariot accident, a car-crash.[25]

In action, the high-performance horse needed not only special exercise and training but in addition to pasturage, hay, grain and other fodder not needed by the less demanding hay-eating ox. Identification is difficult but Kikulli specifies three cereal additives to the hay: two kinds of grain, probably wheat and barley, and meal or groats (as well as salt).[26] In the *Odyssey*, Telemachus and his company unharnessed their chariot horses, leant the vehicles against the wall as we saw, 'and put down fodder before them and mixed white millet with it' (*Od.* 4,41), and straw and barley were provided for Solomon's horses in the tenth century BC (I Kings, 4,28). The classical ration for a cavalry horse given by Polybius was about 1.6 kg (3½ lbs) of barley a day.[27] In China, with the introduction of chariotry in the twelfth century BC as we shall see, there was also later introduced a new fodder crop for the horses, lucern, in the first century BC.[28] Such fodder requirements could draw quite heavily on cereal resources, especially in simple agricultural communities. In the instance of late prehistoric Britain I estimated that, knowing approximate crop yields, a single pair of chariot horses would need the annual consumption crop of barley from 8 to 10 acres (3–4 ha) a year.

Finally, when these requirements of what were no more than essential back-up facilities had been provided for, the driving of the chariot with its trained and mettlesome pair of horses demanded a skilled charioteer, whether for solemn parade and festive or ritual display, or for the more risky exploits of hunting or war. Here the close team-work necessary between high-ranking warrior and passenger meant that the two were often of equal social status, with the emergence in the armies of the great states of *corps d'élite* like that of the Akkadian *mariannu*, the member of the nobility who was a charioteer, or the Egyptian land-owning officer class who also fought from chariots.

This then is what became by the early second millennium BC the expensive package-deal offered to those seeking power and prestige and able to pay for it; it was a deal involving not only things but people. As Robert Drews put it recently:

When...an ambitious...prince acquired chariotry for himself, he did not simply purchase vehicles. He also acquired teams of trained chariot horses; but even good horses and good chariots would by themselves have been useless. The most important ingredient would have been the men who knew how to repair the vehicles, to care for the horses, to drive them in battle, and to fight from a fast-moving chariot.[29]

This is the recent assessment by a classical scholar, independent of my own, but it concerns the chariot solely as a war-engine, a function which has come to overshadow all others. I hope though to show that as a prestige vehicle for the aristocracy it had other important uses, which may have been primary and for pleasure, devoted to public display in procession and parade, in the ceremonial hunt in the royal parks and, less pretentiously, to acting like those eighth-century Greek colonists at Cumae, who went native and 'continually wore gold ornaments and adopted gaily coloured clothes, and rode into the country with their wives in two-horse chariots'.[30] Throughout we are in a familiar world of prestige demonstrated by conspicuous consumption, a formalized drama demanding actors and spectators, the former displaying the tangible and expensive proof of their ascendancy, the latter enjoying the spectacle and the gratification of the symbolic reassurance given of their good fortune in having such potent and auspicious monarchs or gods.

Origins and dispersal

The use of the two-horse chariot as a vehicle of prestige in peace and war for two millennia, from Shang China to Celtic Britain and from the Nile to the Indus, immediately poses the problem of simple or multiple origins on the one hand, and on the other the mechanism or mechanisms whereby what I have called an expensive technological package-deal should be adopted by such diverse societies over such varied terrain. The first question, that of origins, has recently been discussed with concise lucidity by Roger Moorey.[31] He points out that two suggestions have been put forward, that of Mary Littauer and Joost Crouwel, and that which I have offered myself. In the first, the argument is for 'the local evolution of the light, spoked-wheeled, horse-drawn chariot in the Near East itself' and not, as has often been claimed in the past, an introduction from the northern steppe areas. Littauer and Crouwel would see the essential technological innovation of the spoked wheel as evolving from the also openwork and composite but clumsier 'cross-bar' type known from the late third millennium BC on seals from Tepe Hissar in Iran and *c*.2000–1850 BC at Kültepe in Anatolia. The chariot would then have been taken up as a new vehicle form by a large number of disparate societies, as had at an earlier date the disc-wheeled ox-wagon and cart, of which the chariot was a constructionally lighter and, with horse draught, a swifter version, developed initially in the early civilized communities of the Near East.[32]

My alternative view I still think has something to be said in its favour. Given that the natural habitat of the wild horse and its early domestication was on the South Russian steppe, the ancient Near East was at the southern edge of a larger area. Here the first experiments were made in light spoke-wheeled vehicles, a technological reservoir on which Mesopotamia could draw, and then create the chariot, and its later development of organized chariotry and chariot-warfare, which a sophisticated political setting alone could make possible.[33] The simpler 'barbarian' societies could provide circumstances in which the use of light horse-drawn vehicles could sporadically become fashionable and socially accepted, as the archaeological evidence shows, from the Urals and the Caucasus in the mid second millennium BC to south Scandinavia in the early first, and Britain at its end. Adoption of the whole techno-social package-deal in its complex maturity in early Mesopotamia and its neighbour states is another story and a part of international rivalry and the arms race of the early second millennium BC. One thing seems certain, as Moorey says, and that is that

No single ethnic or linguistic group seems to have been the master innovators in the history of horse-drawn light chariotry in the Near Eastern Middle Bronze Age. A diversity of peoples and circumstances more probably explain the gradual incremental change evident in the available, albeit inadequate, range of evidence.[34]

There is a warning here immediately apparent to the archaeologist but perhaps less perceptible to others: we cannot any longer escape from problems, real and imaginary, raised by the linguistic evidence associating horses and chariots uniquely with the Indo-European language group.

The Indo-European minefield

It is here that I am constrained to venture still further into the battle-zone of debate on chariots and tread warily, temerity tempered by timidity, into an intellectual minefield strewn with the corpses of learned reputations, or worse, the still twitching maimed. The trouble seems to have arisen from two main misconceptions. In the first place the undifferentiated horse-drawn light vehicle has been ignored in favour of its specialized Near Eastern use in institutionalized warfare, and has been regarded as inevitably a weapon of aggression and conquest: here the unfortunate overtones of the German word for English 'chariot' and French *char, Streitwagen*, a fighting vehicle, may have contributed an unconscious influence. The second misconception approaches at its worst a myth, and sees horsemanship and chariotry as part of some sort of mystical essence or character with results that have ranged from the politically pernicious to the genially dotty. It is here Moorey's warning applies, and fortunately the archaeologist, linguist and general reader alike can now turn to a sane and balanced view in James Mallory's survey of 1989.[35]

Before turning to the Indo-European languages and to Proto-Indo-European (the linguistically reconstructed parent stock), historical circumstances already described have directed our attention to the Semitic language group, a member of which, Akkadian, became from the beginning of the second millennium BC the dominant language and *lingua franca* of the Near Eastern area in which chariots and chariotry were also making their most significant developments. The Akkadian *narkabtu*, originally a general 'vehicle' word, took on at an early stage the specialized meaning of 'chariot' drawn by horses, as opposed to *sumbu*, a draught wagon drawn by oxen or mules. Behind this is the root *rkb*, a 'conveyance' word, appearing in Ugaritic *mrkbt*, and when Egypt took up the chariot package-deal from Mesopotamia and Syria in the seventeenth century BC, it adopted as a loan-word *mrkbt* for a chariot. In the Levant versions of the same word later appear in Hebrew and Aramaic and it is perhaps significant that Arabic, the language of a people who had from the first repudiated wheeled transport for the camel, uses the same root for both land vehicles and ships: the tired old metaphor of the 'ship of the desert' is literally simply a conveyance on land.[36] Outside this Near Eastern world we encounter Indo-European terminology, unknown linguistic situations, and Chinese, unrelated to any Western language systems.

Mallory has thoroughly reviewed the problem of the Indo-European language group as it stands today. Briefly, as is well known, the widespread distribution of related ancient languages and their recent derviatives demands both the linguistic assumption of an original undifferentiated language which can be inferentially reconstructed as a parent Proto-Indo-European, and that such a language should have become defined in a restricted geographical area (a 'homeland') at an approximate point in time. Simple to state as a thesis, this proposition has engendered an enormous learned and often acrimonious literature which shows little signs of abating. For present purposes I accept with full endorsement Mallory's arguments in favour of an up-to-date re-statement of a position long held probable by linguists and archaeologists, that of a 'homeland' centred on the South Russian steppe from before about 4000 BC. Mallory gives, to my mind, convincing reasons for rejecting two recently presented alternatives, that of Tomas Gamkrelidze and Vyachislav Ivanov for a homeland between east Turkey, the Caucasus and northwest Iran, and Colin Renfrew's for a remote origin in the earliest Neolithic communities of eastern Anatolia. So far as we are concerned with early chariots and speakers of Indo-European languages a fourth-millennium South Russian origin can be accepted, though Drews has recently turned to Gamkrelidze and Ivanov when searching for the origins of Mycenaean chariotry.[37] For the early

Semitic-speaking civilizations, there were a string of non-Indo-European speakers to their north, speaking Hattic in Anatolia, through Hurrian and Kaskian to Urartic in Transcaucasia, but also somewhere, perhaps in northern Iran by the first half of the second millennium BC, people speaking a developed member of the Indo-European language group which was ancestral to the Sanskrit spoken in northwest India by some time before 1000 BC. It was with these peoples that Syria and Mesopotamia came in contact in their quest for the 'equid of the mountains'.

Evidence for the presence of such peoples among the Hurrian-speaking population of North Syria, notably the Mitanni by the fifteenth century BC, is well known.[38] It comes in the form of the names of gods later to be a part of the Vedic Indian pantheon used as witnesses in a fourteenth-century treaty between the Mitannian and Hittite kings; in over a hundred personal names of kings, princes or officials of high rank which again embody Vedic god-names and, significantly for us in the present context, horses and chariots – *Biridashva*, 'owner of great horses', or *Tushratta*, 'he of the terrible chariots', with what was to be the Sanskrit *asva*, a horse, and *ratha*, a chariot. And in the famous horse-training manual referred to earlier on, the Hittite text was taken down by the Mitannian (and so presumably Hurrian speaking) Kikulli, who calls himself 'the horse trainer', *assussani*, the Sanskrit *asvasani*, and uses further proto-Sanskrit technical terms of the numbers of laps run by the horses in his elaborate day-to-day training directions. A considerable Indo-European interest, specifically in speakers of the Indo-Iranian language group, was clearly present among the Hurrian Mitanni and indirectly transmitted to Indo-European Hittites of a separate language group; owing to the fact that Hittite texts are in cuneiform script which uses ideograms as well as logograms and we do not know now how that language vocalized the Sumerian-based ideograms for 'horse' and 'chariot' rendered in Semitic Akkadian as *assisu* and *narkabtu* respectively.

The Indo-European involvement in the earliest chariot-using, that in Mesopotamia and Syria, cannot be traced before the middle of the second millennium BC, and then specifically between the developed Indo-Iranian language group and Hurrian. The intimate linkage between Proto-Indo-Europeans and the horse and chariot is a myth. As long ago as 1957 the linguist Ronald Crossland wrote that 'archaeologists now doubt whether the Indo-Europeans already had the chariot, as distinct from heavier vehicles which could have been drawn by oxen. There is no inherited word for it, or for any part of it which a cart could not have, and there is no philological proof that any Indo-Europeans had it before *c.*1450 BC'.[39] And more recently, Mallory has quoted the Russian historian Igor Diakonov as seeing 'no case for employing the first appearance of the domestic horse and chariot as an ethnic marker for Indo-European migrations'.[40] As for the Indo-European 'homeland' and the wild horse, the fact that they may have coincided or overlapped may be no more than a zoogeographical accident.

Chariots at large

Having emerged from the linguistic minefield (I hope unscathed) it now only remains for us to consider briefly the regional manifestations of the light horse-drawn vehicle in Europe and Asia in the second and first millennia BC. Taking up the distinction made earlier between the unspecialized use of chariot-type vehicles among unsophisticated and simpler societies, and institutionalized chariotry, the product of early urban civilizations, it is convenient to begin with the former, archaeologically known to have a wide range in time and space, from Transcaucasia and the southern Urals to Britain, and again in northwest India.

Continental Europe

I set out the evidence for this area in detail in 1983, and so can briefly summarize it here.[41] Beginning with Transcaucasia as nearest to the civilized ancient Orient, the ox-wagon and cart-burials as prestige offerings in the tombs by Lake Sevan in Armenia have been commented on in Chapter I, and the same burials also included two chariots and the wheel from a third, as well as horse bones. The builders of these tombs were non-urban bronze-using agriculturalists who built hillforts in the mountains adjacent to the lake edge and the cemeteries, with walls of massive undressed blocks like those of their chariot-using Celtic counterparts in later prehistoric western Europe.[42] The date for the chariots (and the bronze models found in the graves) is around 1500 BC and could indicate derivation from the Mitanni or more likely, in view of the unique multi-spoked wheel technology paralleled only in China, be a local development with indigenous horses.

The same must surely apply to evidence from further to the north and west. At Saratov on the Volga a chariot is incised on a pot of

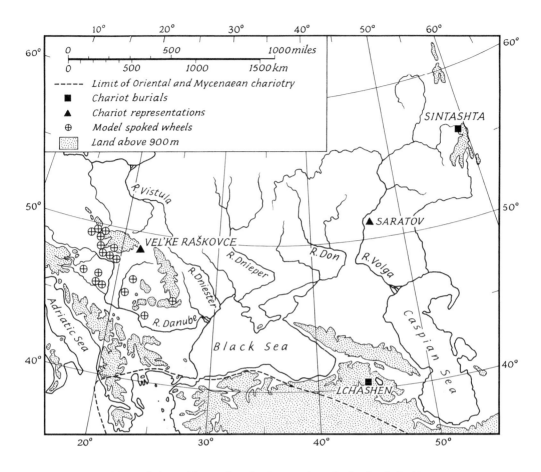

7 Map of the evidence for chariots and spoked wheels in Europe
in the second millennium BC.

the local Timber Grave culture (with dates *c*.1900–1750 BC), and at a cemetery on the Sintashta River in the southern Urals are chariot-burials with ten-spoked wheels and horse sacrifices. Westwards in Czechoslovakia are pottery spoked-wheel models of the local Bronze Age *c*.2000–1900 BC and on a slightly later (*c*.1700) pot an incised frieze of processional chariots and horses, and horse bones appear in kitchen refuse from settlements of *c*.2600–1900 BC. We are here in the territory of Bökönyi's Western group of horse, and bones of wild horses appear in quantity in late Neolithic settlements in south Germany about 3600–3400 BC. In the recent past many archaeologists interpreted this chariot evidence in barbarian Bronze Age Europe as derived from the Mycenaean world, a rather romantic view hardly tenable today especially in face of the calibrated radiocarbon dates just quoted.[43] It is far better seen as a diffuse barbarian phenomenon of the use of chariots as prestige vehicles worthy of burial (in the Urals) or depiction in processional use (Slovakia). This tradition appears later, probably not before the twelfth century BC, in rock carvings of chariots in Scandinavia and north Italy, and finally, in northwestern Europe, from the seventh-century Hallstatt C phase, when prestige two-wheeled horse-drawn chariots appear as grave offerings, up to the equivalent chariot-graves of the last couple of centuries BC in Yorkshire, and literary evidence of chariot warfare takes us in North Britain up to the third century AD. The linguistic affiliations of these areas of chariot usage are unknown, except for the Indo-European Celtic languages of central and northwest Europe from the sixth century BC. In the Gallo-Britonnic language at the end of the first century BC, various names were given to the chariot, in their Latin forms *covinnus, essedum* and *carpentum* (see Chapter I), the last giving the Old Irish *carpat*.[44]

A separate chariot-using tradition in the barbarian Mediterranean is that transmitted as a part of the orientalizing movement from Cypriot and broadly speaking Phoenician sources in the Aegean and the Levant westwards from the eighth century BC, represented in North Africa by the well-known rock art of the Saharan Atlas Mountains, and the memorial stelae of southwest Iberia.[45] If any languages other than those indigenous to these regions were to be involved, they would have been Semitic.

Vedic India and the Aryans

An indisputable and remarkable example of the use of the chariot by a barbarian Indo-European society is that of the first Sanskrit-speaking newcomers into the northwest of the Indian subcontinent at the end of the second millennium BC. We saw earlier in this chapter that there was linguistic evidence of peoples somehow mixed up in the horse trade of the Hurrians of North Syria in the fourteenth century who spoke an Indic branch of the Indo-European languages, to become Aryan Sanskrit in India and Avestan Persian in Iran. We can use the baleful word 'Aryan' here without trepidation, as it was what they called themselves – *aryas*, just simply The Best, as in the cognate Greek *aristos*. They have no identifiable material culture and the date of their arrival and settlement in India is now seen as subsequent to, but fairly certainly unconnected with, the decay and fall of the urban civilization of the Indus about the middle of the second millennium. A date within the centuries 1200–1000 BC would seem reasonable. These Aryans are known only by their own surviving and originally orally transmitted retrospective religious texts, the Vedas and their congeners, and the extraction from these confused works of pious myth, traditional ritual imperfectly understood, and speculative allegory, of any commonsense facts of social structure or technology is intimidatingly difficult, nor does the deep-seated anhistoric ethos of ancient India help matters.

We can however quickly perceive that Vedic society was the antithesis of urban civility; it was that of simple bronze- or copper-working agriculturalists in small communities with domesticated animals, including cattle herded in quantities and valued as status symbols to be accumulated as the prized booty of intertribal raiding between petty chieftains. High value was also set on the horse, as the essential traction animal of the equally prestigious chariot, in which chieftains paraded and fought with bows and arrows, and took part in elaborate religious ceremonies, particularly in ritual chariot racing. In all, a barbarian society not dissimilar from that of the Celtic-speaking peoples of northwest Europe of the last centuries BC, at the other end of the ancient world.

The Vedic chariot can be reconstructed from the texts in some detail, and my own interpretation of forty years ago has stood the test of time surprisingly well.[46] The vehicle seems to have been of normal Near Eastern type and was known as *ratha*, a wheel-word cognate with Latin *rota* or German *rad*; for the wheel itself another Indo-European alternative was used, *cakra* (Greek *kuklos*, English 'wheel'). Other parts are specified such as draught pole, body or box, yoke, the yoke-lashings and the components of the spoked wheel including the felloe which we know to have been bent in one piece, *nemi*. We saw that the chariot was placed on a 'stand' to avoid distortion of the wheels. The specialized craftsman who built and repaired chariots was *ratha-kara* and such chariots were drawn by a pair of horses (*asva*); there is no mention of bits, but a phrase 'control of the nostrils' could imply nose-rings in the manner of the early Near Eastern equid harnessing.

As for its use and social status, the Vedic *ratha* was certainly the prerogative of chieftains ('kings') and their entourage of archer-warriors. The liturgical texts from which our information comes naturally stress its use in religious and ceremonial performances, especially the ritual chariot races, but much is also made of chariot warfare, with arrows shot while still on the move, against the subjected (and probably Dravidian-speaking) native population, and among rival Aryan chiefs in cattle-raiding, which seems to have been regarded in the same terms as hunting as an upper-class sport. But as the most recent Vedic study makes clear, if in the first place we envisage the Aryans as 'semi-nomadic tribes migrating towards the East with their cattle' there is no 'logical or natural connection' between this and chariotry, for 'it is difficult to imagine how the chariot might have been used for cattle-tending or cattle-conquering ... it is at any rate unclear in what way the chariot would have been of immediate use to cattle-raiders, for whom horse riding would seem to be far more practical.'[47]

The chariot package-deal taken up: the Near East

Having dealt with the chariot as the vehicle of prestige – the only approved conveyance for the chieftain and his noble entourage in ceremony and ritual, hunting and its counterpart, warfare – in societies of lesser sophistication than those of the urban cultures of the second millennium BC, we may now turn to make a brief review of how the more complex package-deal was adopted and maintained by these Near Eastern civilizations. Here the textual evidence is direct and factual, in a context of literate societies that are historical entities with geographical and political boundaries, enabling us to take in order the Babylonian and Assyrian, and thence the Egyptian, the Levantine and the Hittite worlds, followed by Mycenaean Greece and its Homeric reflection, and finally China of the Shang and Zhou dynasties. In all these the economic and political structure of the state was of a competence and temper to stand the expense of an organization of transport for the delectation of its rulers in display and ostentation, ceremonial and ritual, the sport of hunting and – the one merging psychologically with the other – increasingly in state warfare. This was, for over half a millennium, the age of High Chariotry, the counterpart of the Age of Chivalry in the western European Middle Ages.

An outline of the state and temple organization for chariotry can be gained from Akkadian texts of the second half of the second millennium BC.[48] The chariot crew was normally two, the charioteer or 'master of the chariot' and 'the second man in the chariot' who was the warrior, classed as a *mariannu*, 'primarily as a noble who is a chariot-warrior', together forming a *corps d'élite* with a name which is a loan-word from Indo-Aryan with the sense of 'young man'. The Egyptians took up the package-deal complete with the chariot-word derived from Akkadian as we saw, and their texts give greater details of the military set-up.[49] The army consisted of infantry and chariotry together, the chariots in units of 10 with a maximum strength at any one time of about 50: the ratio of chariots to infantry under Ramesses IV was 50 to 5,000. The army ranks comprised the chariot warrior, a gentleman from the landowning class, and the charioteer and shield-bearer, as we have seen, of equal or even superior rank. Stables and stores were under the civilian authorities and no doubt had a staff of grooms and stable-lads as well as quartermasters and their clerks to check the issues (as in the Mycenaean palaces). These would have included the grain ration in barley, not in fact very suitable for horses as apt to induce short-windedness and sweating until digestive tolerance is achieved,[50] but universal in recorded antiquity until the adoption of the northern fodder-grain oats in early medieval northwest Europe.

We know little in detail of the chariotry of the Hittites beyond its extensive deployment in war: they had clearly taken up the package-deal from the Near East, probably from the Mitannian area, perhaps from the seventeenth and certainly by the fifteenth century BC. Chariot tactics on the battlefield are the province of the military historian,[51] but the massed chariot charge is a fiction, and ostentatious parade and intimidation, mobile command posts and flanking actions seem the chariot's main function, with bow and arrow or light throwing spear as mobile missiles: if swords and heavy spears and body armour were involved, earlier chariotry provided a quick delivery and rescue service to and from the field of battle.

But the great civil demonstration of the monarch as charioteer was in the Royal Hunt, carried out in open country or, increasingly from the second millennium BC onwards, in royal hunting parks set aside and enclosed as game reserves. These, in the Near East and again in China, began a tradition which was to lie behind the European medieval parks and forests set aside for royal enjoyment.

pls. 1,2 In the hunting reliefs of Assurbanipal (669–626 BC) one shows the pursuit of wild onagers: in the Byzantine Imperial Park near Constantinople, Luidprand Bishop of Cremona on his embassy from the Emperor Otto in AD 968 was shown not only deer but wild asses, perhaps also onagers.[52] In the second-millennium Near East the most

pl. 4 famous scene of the king hunting from his chariot is Tutankhamun's lion hunt painted on the lid of a casket from his tomb of the mid fourteenth century; rather earlier is the chariot hunt for wild cattle on a gold bowl from Ugarit (Ras Shamra). Later the hunting scenes of lions in the parks of Assurbanipal mentioned above are justly famous (in one a lion is being let out of a cage for the king to slay, like a bag-fox at a Victorian hunt).[53] We shall encounter the chariot with the deer and boar hunts in Mycenaean Greece and again in the royal hunting parks of Shang China.

The Hebrews of the Israelite monarchy took up the package-deal so far as it concerned warfare and added chariot units to their infantry forces from the time of David about 975 BC and Solomon, 950–925 BC. By this time chariotry is about to give way to the ridden horse for the king in battle: cavalry is taking over in Assyria from the time of Assurnasirpal (883–859 BC) and Shalmaneser III (858–824 BC) is shown on horseback on the bronze-bound gates of Balawat. These changed circumstances of the prestige of the ridden horse will be taken up in the next chapter.[54]

The Greeks and their chariot deal

At an earlier point in this chapter we took a look at the barbarian use of the chariot in continental Europe while reserving the peculiar circumstances of the Greek peninsula and the Aegean, where in Crete and on the mainland the Minoan and Mycenaean civilizations take their place as east-Mediterranean extensions of the palace- and temple-centred urban civilizations earlier established in the Near East, the Levant and Egypt. As a part of their political and economic structure such societies needed writing; scripts were therefore devised to record the spoken word. That (or those) of Crete remains undeciphered (Linear A and 'hieroglyphic'); the Linear B script written on clay tablets dating from about 1400 BC at Knossos and

1200 BC in mainland Greece was that adopted by the Mycenaeans to write what, since its decipherment by Michael Ventris in the 1950s, is now recognized as an early form of the Greek language.

Here we are again on the edge of one of the most dangerous parts of the linguistic minefield, the origins of the Greek language and the date and circumstances of its first appearance in the geographical area of ancient and modern Greece. 'The coming of the Greeks' is a phrase fraught with not only scholarly, but for many emotional, significance as a part of the Greek mystique so deeply engrained in the Western consciousness.[55] For our present purposes let us remember that the presence or knowledge of horses does not presuppose the existence or use of chariots, and that neither animal nor vehicle is exclusively associated with any language group. Here we are only incidentally concerned with language origins or transmission, but directly with the circumstances of the acquisition of what I have called the package-deal involved in setting up some form of institutionalized chariotry as an instrument of status transport by the Aegean palatial power centres. Two main theses have been set out in recent years: that of Joost Crouwel in 1981, seeing Mycenaean chariotry as an extension westwards of the oriental traditions of Mesopotamia, Syria and Egypt, and that of Robert Drews of 1988, taking it to be the military means whereby Indo-European invaders established themselves and their language as the first Greeks.[56] Both of course represent viewpoints that embody the work of previous scholars in both approaches, but present new syntheses. Let us briefly review the evidence.

First, the horse. Greece is not potential wild horse territory but is adjacent to such in the European north and the Anatolian east. As we saw, wild horses were present by about 3000 BC at Demirci Hüyük at the western end of the Anatolian steppe and at Troy, 330 km (200 miles) west again, horse bones appear in Troy VI (*c.*1850–1300 BC) in kitchen refuse of animals of Bökönyi's Eastern group, which have sometimes without justification been associated with chariot draught. In Greece itself there is good evidence from domestic rubbish of horse bones from Middle Helladic (beginning of second millennium) to Late Helladic (Mycenaean) times from sites such as Lerna and Nichoria, representing animals around 140 cm tall and, in a Mycenaean example from Lerna, one of the Eastern group standing at 145 cm. Paired horse-burials from four sites (Marathon, Dara, Dendra, Paros) appear to be Mycenaean but have few details and no osteological reports: they would compare with the equid pairs from earlier Mesopotamia. Bones of donkeys have a similar range of dates in Greece and there may be a horse × donkey cross from Lerna. Horses as potential traction animals were therefore around in Greece from early in the second millennium BC.[57]

For the chariot and its use we turn first to iconography: no burials or other archaeological finds enlighten us. From the Shaft Graves at Mycenae, which with their splendour and novelty mark a dynasty founding the Late Helladic period in the seventeenth century BC,

pl. 5 come carved stone stelae representing men, one carrying a sword, in chariots drawn by clumsily depicted beasts which suggest that the sculptor was more familiar with bulls and lions than horses. A gold signet ring from one grave is engraved with two men, charioteer and archer, hunting a stag in hilly landscape from a chariot drawn by two lively horses in the conventional 'flying gallop' pose. Other chariot representations on seals, painted pots and wall paintings show how Mycenaean chariot design took on distinctive local forms unknown in the adjacent Near East; none represents scenes of battles conducted from moving vehicles nor of bowmen, but rituals including women or deities in procession; hunting scenes with participants and spectators (including the young ladies at Tiryns) or taken to the battle which is then conducted on foot; a single fragmentary scene of chariot racing. The pictographs used with the Linear B syllabary on the palace inventory tablet show further schematic renderings of chariots and wheels consonant with those from the other sources. They record an interesting detail of harnessing, the 'yoke saddle' at the horse's withers or neck, a feature also found in Egypt, Mesopotamia, China and Pazyryk in the Altai,[58] but not in the Caucasus or in continental Europe. In sum, Crouwel sees that 'the vehicles were valued as a relatively fast, prestigious means of conveyance' in civil and military contexts. In the latter, archery from the chariot in the manner of the Egyptians or the Vedic Aryans was not practised, but the vehicle would bring a warrior armed with sword and spear (and on occasion heavily corseleted) to the field of battle as to the hunt, there to engage the foe or the quarry. Such chariot use might be reflected by Hittite tactics at Kadesh (c.1286 BC) and form a genuine reminiscence in the eighth-century *Iliad*. In civil use, the importance of hunting as a part of oriental chariotry has already been seen, as have ceremonial and religious processions and, most interesting in this context, the ritual chariot-racing of Vedic India.

The lexical evidence for chariots and their horses afforded by the Mycenaean Greek of the Linear B tablets from Knossos about 1400 BC and Pylos a couple of centuries later, has formed the storm-centre of the debate on the transmission on the one hand of the language and on the other the technological complex of chariotry, into the Aegean of the second millennium BC.[59] It must be said once more that the technology is independent of linguistic considerations: to repeat Roger Moorey, 'no single ethnic or linguistic group seems to have been the master innovator', and Igor Diakonov, that there is 'no case for employing the first appearance of the domestic horse and chariot' as indicative of Indo-European speakers. It is also noteworthy that among the peoples using institutionalized chariotry adjacent to the Aegean were those speaking Semitic and allied languages as well as Hurrian, and of the two Indo-European languages in the same context, the Hittite group are not closely related to Greek. As Martin Bernal has recently and rightly reminded us, though an Indo-European language, Greek is not the Indo-Aryan known to the Mitannian horse-trainers and in the Vedic tradition of chariot-using.[60]

When we turn to the chariot vocabulary in Mycenaean we can straight away set aside the terms such as wheel, axle, yoke, paired animal draught and unspecified vehicles since these are, as Crossland pointed out, all equally applicable to the oxen or equid-drawn conveyances of antiquity. The horse has a name, *i-qo*, Greek *hippos*, from the Proto-Indo-European root which gives the cognate Indo-Aryan *asva*: it may be significant that the word for a donkey, Mycenaean *o-no*, Greek *onos*, belongs to a non-Indo-European substrate, appropriate to a long established Asiatic domesticate. The chariot itself is called by an abbreviation, the adjectival *i-qi-ja*, 'horsey', presupposing a noun such as *wo-ka*, a vehicle or conveyance, from the Proto-Indo-European that incidentally gives these two English words, in a usage comparable to the modern English 'motor' for 'motor car', where the propulsive force is the distinctive feature. As we saw, the Indo-Aryan usage is quite different, where *ratha* for a chariot stresses that it moves on wheels. The mental set behind the chariot concept in Greek was therefore distinct from that in Sanskrit, and both from Semitic, where a generalized conveyance word was rendered specific in usage. As we saw, the use of cuneiform ideograms deprives us of the Hittite words for horse and chariot, and when we shortly turn to China we shall see that no language transmission accompanied the adoption of the chariot. What is clear from the Linear B inventories is that at the time of their use chariotry as an organized institution of warfare and probably ceremonial and ritual was being state supported and managed in the same manner as in the contemporary Near Eastern or Egyptian civilizations. The 'oriental' quality of the inferred Minoan and Mycenaean palace and temple political structure has often been commented on, and it is no surprise to find chariotry common to all. The question remains as to how and in what circumstances this occurred in Crete and Greece.

It is here that Robert Drews's recent interpretation of the evidence has to be taken into account. He would see the appearance of the Greek language and organized chariotry in the Aegean in the second millennium BC as inseparably linked, and the latter as the means by which the former was forcibly introduced in an invasive conquest by the founders of the Shaft Grave dynasty at the opening of the Late Helladic period. The origin of the peoples involved – the first Greeks – he would seek (following the linguists Gamkrelidze and Ivanov) in eastern Anatolia and Armenia, and bring them to Greece by sea along the south coast of the Black Sea, where they established themselves as overlords among the Middle Helladic population by the offensive use of chariot warfare. This 'takeover', as he sees it, he compares with the Indo-Aryan incursion of the Indian subcontinent.

Initially persuasive – the Shaft Graves have long been recognized as archaeologically indicative of some dynastic discontinuity with exterior contacts beyond Minoan Crete – the evidence may perhaps be read in an alternative way. In the first place we have seen no reason to equate languages with chariots, and certainly not with Indo-European; the Greek language and the Aegean use of the chariot need not necessarily be linked. Comparison with the Indo-Aryan movements ignores the differences I have tried to set out between the inchoate use of the chariot by barbarian societies and that of institutionalized state-supported chariotry. Drews is well aware of this and I quoted his apposite description of what I have called the chariot package-deal. Can we not see the Aegean situation in this way? The Shaft Grave dynasty, however established, by internal climax or from outside, formed a new up-and-coming little state emulating the older and greater civilizations to its east. It may have used chariots from the first, but of the Shaft Grave representations the gold intaglio ring with an archery stag-hunting scene, and the stelae, with the 'warrior beneath the chariot-horses' hoofs' motif, are both well-known oriental stock scenes, visual topoi, artistic clichés, which may not represent Mycenaean actuality. If we do not, in Drews's words, envisage 'a takeover of Greece by a charioteering community who came from the lands south of the Caucasus'[61] and separating language from vehicle technology, can we see it in another way? We might envisage Mycenaean Greece, as a part of establishing its new status, adopting the contemporary prestige symbol of state-run organized chariotry from one of its eastern neighbours, taking up the package-deal with its commitments and its reputation. If languages are in any way to be considered, one might see no more than the Indo-European Greeks keeping up with the Semitic Joneses.

The Chinese phenomenon

Discussions of ancient chariotry tend to omit the phenomenon of China,[62] where from late in the Shang dynasty, about 1200 BC, the two-horse chariot quite suddenly appears in the archaeology and the earliest Chinese texts as a vehicle of royal prestige for hunting, ritual parade and warfare. This last use declined by the end of the Zhou dynasty (1027–771 BC) and cavalry begins to supplant chariotry with the introduction of horse-riding to China, traditionally in 307 BC, and stirrups appear in the fourth century AD. Shang chariotry appears to mark the first appearance of any wheeled transport in the area which was to become the nucleus of Imperial China on the Yellow River; plough agriculture is not attested until the mid fourth century BC, in the period of the Warring States (483–221 BC). Clearly we have a very different background for the use of the chariot than anything in Western Asia or Europe; equally clearly we must seek the origins of the horse-drawn chariot outside China, to the west and north.[63]

Chariot origins
The numerous chariot-burials of the Shang and Zhou date, admirably excavated and published, give us full details of vehicle technology, and these direct our attention to the chariot burials of Transcaucasia of *c.*1500 BC already mentioned. Although 6500 km away on the 40° parallel to the west, their typological peculiarities are so closely akin to the Chinese counterparts that connection is inevitable, the more so since they are also so unlike contemporary Near Eastern types. Here I feel bound to disagree with the reconstruction of the chariots by the Armenian archaeologists about which I have earlier expressed partial reservations. The two chariots found at Lchashen had been buried incomplete, without their draught-poles or yokes, as body-wheels-and-axle units. The draught-pole was subsequently restored, in the museum at Erevan and in the published drawings, as a modern

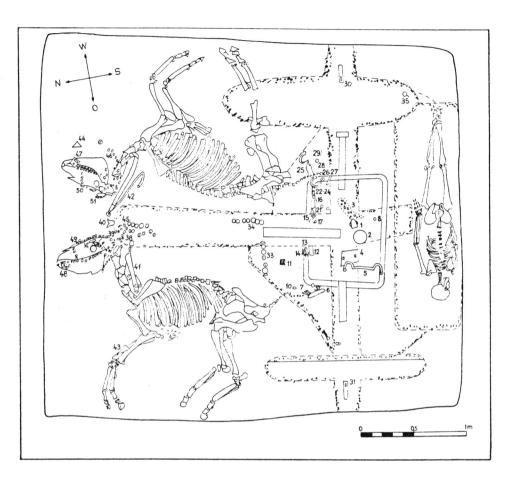

8 Plan of Shang Dynasty chariot burial at Da-si-gong-zun, China.

straight rod, itself an impossible means of harnessing, on which the body was set open at the front and railed at back and sides – an arrangement unparalleled in ancient chariots. I propose now that we disregard the modern reconstruction and assume the original draught-pole to have been curved in the normal manner to rise to withers height at the yoke, and the body to be reversed on its axle, with rails to the front and sides. With this important modification the Lchashen chariot becomes even closer to the Chinese type than before. The multi-spoked bent-felloe wheels are the first and most distinctive feature, with 28 spokes as against the Western Asiatic 4 or later 8, but comparable with the Chinese 18 to 26 in Shang, 18 to 30 in Zhou chariots; the wheel gauge is 170 cm (Shang 215–240 cm; Zhou 164–244 cm) and the shallow-fronted wide body or box, as against the normal high-fronted Near Eastern type, 100 by 50 cm as compared with Shang 129 by 74 cm or Zhou 140 by 60 cm. We have no evidence for the yoke arrangement at Lchashen, but Chinese practice used the yoke saddle as in Egypt and Mycenaean Greece (and as we shall see later in the Altai and in Central Asian rock-carvings). In all, an adoption by the Chinese, in late Shang times, of the horse-drawn chariot from their barbarian neighbours to the west seems demanded by the archaeological evidence, while the texts show how its use was formalized into state-sponsored chariotry in a process parallel to, but quite independent of, the western developments we have sketched earlier on. Chinese chariotry was a Chinese 'package' created on the Yellow River from the basic horse-and-chariot technological prerequisite, acquired incidentally without any linguistic affiliations, Semitic or Indo-European.

Some 1600 km north of Lchashen in the southern Urals the Sintashta River chariot burials have 10-spoked vehicles of light construction and horse remains; further eastwards rock carvings of chariots and horses, undated but probably second to first millennium BC, occur in southern Kazakhstan, Tadzhikstan, and Outer Mongolia, some with yoke saddles.[64] In the High Altai some 3000 km northwest of the Shang kingdom, at Pazyryk in Barrow 5, of the fifth-century BC cemetery with its graves miraculously preserved in permafrost conditions, a great four-wheeled ceremonial carriage survived intact and is further described in Chapter IV. Its huge wheels, 1.6 m in diameter, have single-piece bent felloes and 34 spokes and a gauge of 2.5 m. They are of birch wood (as is the whole vehicle) with birch-bark binding as in the Egyptian chariots, and it has yoke-saddles.[65] It has sometimes been considered as a Chinese import but it could well represent an indigenous tradition of coach-building in the vast area between the Caucasus and the Yellow River from which Shang China derived its chariot technology. The 12-spoked wheel from the Xiong-nu cemetery of Noin-ula, in northern Mongolia 130 km north of Ulan Bator and of the first century AD, may in fact be Chinese of the Han dynasty.[66]

The horses
The wild horse was not native to China proper, but as we saw the last Przewalsky's horses were sighted in Outer Mongolia. We have unfortunately no osteological reports on the horses from the Chinese chariot burials, but at the outset they must have been imports, ponies of about 135 cm withers height, and wild horses were kept in the royal Shang hunting parks, where they were captured by netting, perhaps with intent to tame and breed them. But the evidence from the Pazyryk graves just mentioned, where horses were buried and preserved by frost, shows that by the fifth century BC in that region not only such horses, but a superior type was present with all the qualities of Bökönyi's Eastern group which we saw went back to the sixteenth century BC as an import into Egypt and Anatolia, and have the characteristics of the modern 'Arab'; 'larger... with relatively shorter backs, longer and slenderer legs, a longer narrower head with convex, rather than straight or concave profile, and finer coats'.[67] The Chinese, keeping up the standards of the Imperial Studs, clearly sought good horses from their barbarian neighbours to the north and west, and in the late second century BC, reports came through of the fine horses of Da Yuan or Ferghana, east of Tashkent, 3500 km westwards along what became the course of the ancient Silk Route. These were the famous Heavenly Horses, and whether or not they sweated blood and were sired by dragons in lakes, they were the object of diplomatic negotiations and military campaigns by the Emperor Wu from 115 BC, culminating in 101 when a triumphal hymn, perhaps written by the Emperor, announced:

> The Heavenly Horses are coming
> Coming from the Far West
> They crossed the Flowing Sands
> For the barbarians are conquered,
> The Heavenly Horses are coming...

They were indeed – 30 'superior' animals and 3000 of 'middling or lower quality' – and Arthur Waley showed that these were swift chariot ponies to take the Emperor to the abode of the Immortals: in fact 'Eastern group' horses to be seen as such in contemporary art and not, as many have thought, heavy cavalry. From Ferghana too were brought back seeds of lucern (*Medicago sativa*), a leguminous fodder plant appropriate to the better stock, which was then extensively grown in China.

The chariot displayed

From the earliest Chinese texts, the divinatory Oracle Bones of the eleventh century BC, the chariot appears as a royal adjunct to ceremonial display, hunting and courtly warfare. The texts, the first Chinese literature, record the brief aphoristic replies to oracular enquiry from the pattern of cracks on pieces of heated bone, usually animal shoulder-blades, a widespread form of ancient divination. One records the outcome of a dubious omen in the hunting field: 'The king went out in chase of rhinoceros. The Minor Vassal harmed the chariot and horse, overturning the king's chariot; Prince Yang also fell out.' The chariot clearly held three; the king, the prince and the Minor Vassal as the unfortunately inept charioteer, a title used more than once. The hunt would have been in one of the royal parks or game reserves and other texts refer to deer and wild horses as quarry. The Imperial Hunting Park at Peking survived until the end of the Manchu Empire and it was there, in 1865, that the Abbé Armand David sighted the last surviving herd of *milou* deer since named after him. Apart from half-a-dozen divinations referring to chariots used in hunting, and one in ritual, a couple refer to war against barbarians on the northern border who also seem to be using chariots. Later texts show how within China warfare at the aristocratic level was conducted as between chivalrous gentlemen, with an agreed battlefield prepared by levelling up irregularities of the ground to avoid accidents on either side. In general the chariots in war were a spectacular demonstration of power and magnificence and as mobile command platforms for military leaders. As we saw, cavalry took over from the fourth century BC, and thereafter the chariot became increasingly an aristocratic pleasure carriage until well into Han times.

Draught was with a pair of yoked horses with yoke saddles in Shang times, but in later Zhou four horses were harnessed, two under the yoke and two flanking with traces. By AD 200 shaft harnessing with a breast strap was in use, and by the fifth century with a rigid horse-collar, ancestral to subsequent developments in the west. Throughout, the Chinese chariot was a vehicle of delight and display, for pleasure and vanity, pomp and command. From the tenth century BC Zhou inscriptions record in detail the royal conferral of chariots or chariot equipment as marks of favour and insignia of office: 'a chariot of bronze fittings with a decorated cover on the handrail; a front rail and breast-trappings for the horses of soft leather, painted scarlet; a canopy of tiger-skin, with a reddish-brown lining...bells for the yoke-bar...a gilt bow-press and a fish-skin quiver; harness for a team of four horses; gilt bridles and girth-straps...'

And in the poems of the Book of Odes, around 800–600 BC (and so contemporary with Homer and Hesiod, but in how different a world!), the lyrical enumeration of the chariot trappings and its steeds conveys the exuberance of sheer pleasure in elegance –

> The small war-chariot with its shallow body
> The upturned chariot-pole with its five bands,
> The slip-rings, the flank-checks,
> The traces stowed away in their silver case,
> The patterned mat, the long hubs,
> Drawn by our piebalds, our whitefoots...
> The four steeds so strong
> The six reins in his hands
> The piebald and the bay with the black mane are outside,
> The brown horse with black mouth and the deep black horse
>   are outside.[68]

III
Princes on Horseback

'No animal is more noble than the horse, since it is by horses that princes, magnates and knights are separated from lesser people, and because a lord cannot fittingly be seen among private citizens except through the mediation of a horse.' So, in the high Middle Ages of western Christendom about AD 1250, wrote the Calabrian Jordanus Ruffus, knight-farrier (*miles in marestale*) to the Hohenstaufen Emperor Frederick II.[1] The horse as the ultimate steed of prestige, the only bearer of monarchy in motion, is established after two thousand years of domestication and use, from traction in ceremonial chariotry to a new rôle, as majesty abandoned the vehicle and took the motive power between its own knees.

The East

The beginnings of regal horse-riding were tentative. In the ancient Near Eastern tradition the king, if he did not appear in a chariot, might on occasion ride on a mule or a donkey: in Archaic Egypt from about 3000 BC ritual burials of donkeys accompanied tombs at Tarkhan and Helwan, and singly or in pairs at Tell ed Dab'a in the late seventeenth century BC,[2] and at a similar date in the Hittite Osmanskayasi cemetery. In the early second millennium a well-known letter to Zimri-Lin, King of Mari, gives him advice on this matter – 'Let my lord not ride horses. Let him mount only chariots or mules and honour his kingly head.'[3] A thousand years later Absolom, son of the Israelite king David about 975 BC, is in command of an infantry unit with a chariot corps, but himself rides a mule, while traditional Jewish law put a prohibition on horse-breeding by the king: 'he shall not multiply horses to himself, nor cause the people to return to Egypt to the end that he should multiply horses'

69

(II Sam. 18,9; Deut. 18,6). In the Messianic aspirations of Zechariah 'thy king cometh unto thee... lowly and riding upon an ass, and upon a colt the foal of an ass' (Zech. 9,9), and this was taken up as a fulfilled prophecy and used verbatim of Christ's entry into Jerusalem in John 12,4. The original concept is not of humility but rather an assertion of kingship in the ancient Semitic tradition, but it would only be seen as demeaning by the provincial Graeco-Roman world of the first century AD, where the horse was now firmly established as the steed of majesty and authority, the donkey as the lowly beast of burden.[4]

But as we saw in the last chapter, cavalry was taking over from chariotry in Assyria by the ninth century BC and the king Shalmaneser III (858–824 BC) is depicted as riding on horseback.[5] Thenceforward the monarch as a warrior on horseback became the accepted convention in the ancient Orient. By the seventh century BC momentous re-alignments of power were taking place, and new people with a tradition of mobile horsemanship from the west Asiatic steppe were establishing themselves in the ancient centres of authority; Nineveh was destroyed by the Medes in 606 BC, Babylon conquered by Cyrus, founder of the Persian Achaemenid dynasty, in 539 BC. The tribes known to the Assyrians as the Ishkuzai and Gimirrai (the Scythians and the Cimmerians) were raiding the Caucasian kingdom of Urartu from the time of Sargon II (721–705) and continued their raids of devastation into Asia Minor, the Cimmerians destroying the kingdoms of Phrygia and Lydia before their defeat by Assurbanipal (668–626). The Scythians moved eastwards, establishing themselves round Lake Urmia, where they invaded Median territory in the mid seventh century. These peoples all shared an economic and military structure based on the mastery of the ridden horse and the use of the bow, barbarian and at least partly nomadic in origin but by the time of the Achaemenids integrated into the sophisticated literate civilized culture of ancient Persia. It was this horse-riding Persia that was to confront the Greeks at the end of the fifth century BC, before being itself invaded and conquered by the forces of Alexander, who died in 323 BC. The Greek Seleucid dynasty was established by before 280 BC and maintained until it in turn was superseded by the Parthians, who remained the dominant power in Persia until the beginning of the third century AD, when the Sassanian kings rose to prominence until conquered by the Arabs around AD 650. By this time, in western Christendom, we are in the early Middle Ages. Both east and west at this period were influenced by the steppe tradition of horsemanship transmitted through Persia: the camel-riding Arabs adopted cavalry and the European armoured knight, as we shall see, owed much to older traditions in the Orient.

The use of the chariot in ceremony and war dwindled, with the final use in warfare of the enigmatic scythed chariot, not attested by archaeology or iconography but known only from literary references.[6] The Achaemenid Persians concerned themselves with breeding, especially from Bökönyi's Eastern-group horses, and their comparatively heavy 'long-bodied, big-boned and ram-headed' breed were probably the Median 'Great Nesaean' horses of Herodotus shown on the relief sculpture: like all 'Great Horses' of antiquity these are not likely to have been above 150 cm in height. At the other end of the scale a very small but elegant type, the Caspian Horse, only 100–122 cm in height, represented on reliefs and seals, was 'rediscovered' in 1965 and is now a recognized breed.[7] It was as riders and archers that the Persians were seen by their contemporaries – Herodotus (I, 136) records their maxim for young manhood, 'to ride, to draw the bow and to speak the truth'. The little Hebrew folk-tale preserved in the Old Testament Book of Esther is set in the Achaemenid court of Ahasuerus (Xerxes I, 485–465 BC), and its hero and heroine are Mordecai and Esther, the names of the old Babylonian deities Marduk and Ishtar. When Mordecai is honoured by the king he is given royal robes and 'the horse that the king rideth upon and the crown royal which is set upon his head'.

The Greek and Roman World

In the twelfth century BC the ancient civilizations of the eastern Mediterranean were disrupted and in part destroyed in the circumstances associated with the barbarian raids of the miscellaneous tribes called by the Egyptians the Sea Peoples. Chariotry ended with the cessation of its support-system, and in the new Dark Ages the use of chariots survived only for some ceremonial functions including racing. In the eighth century the Homeric epics, orally transmitted, were set down in their present form, preserving fragments of a Mycenaean past, in the *Iliad* attributed to an engagement at Troy in western Anatolia, centuries before. 'Troy was a city like Miletus, like Tarsus, like Ugarit, that was attacked, ruined and forgotten... a paradigm of many sieges, many quarrels, many fights and many returns' in the days of the brigands, pirates and displaced noblemen of the crack-up of the Aegean in the twelfth century,[8] the tale of which fortuitously survived in heroic legend. The *Iliad*'s horsemanship and chariot warfare is therefore that of late Mycenaean Greece as imagined by the poets five centuries later, and is therefore a very tricky source, as the huge literature about it bears witness. Moses Finley once quoted as a parallel the medieval European military engagement of AD 778 when Charlemagne's expeditionary force returning from Moslem Spain through the Pyrenees was ambushed and massacred by the local Basques at Roncevalles. Centuries later, about 1150, the Anglo-Norman poem the *Chanson de Roland* presents this as an heroic battle fought by Christian knights against 400,000 Saracens.[9]

Improved breeding of horses for chariots and increasingly for individual riding in Greece is shown pictorially by the development of naturalistic art in pottery decoration and sculpture from the seventh century BC. Here it can be recognized that Western- and, particularly for finer animals, Eastern-group horses were being bred from about 700 BC; riding as well as chariot-driving took a place in the Olympic Games from 648 BC though, as usual in antiquity, even the larger horses are unlikely to have been above 150 cm high, and were probably in a minority. By the seventh century cavalry was becoming a component in Greek armies and soon riding was accepted as part of the necessary education of a young gentleman.[10] From the eighth century Greeks were making contacts with horsemanship beyond their own world, with their first colonies in the west such as Pithekoussai and Cumae, and in the east Al Mina at the mouth of the Orontes. After Tiglath-pileser III's conquest of Urartu in 743, Assyrian power was extended westwards to the Mediterranean in Syria and Cilicia, with its cavalry and superior horses.[11] Further to the north the Scythians were establishing themselves within the Carpathian Ring on the Hungarian Plain from the seventh century (and even raiding Egypt in 611), with the Persian Darius pursuing them into Thrace in 512; the Greeks encountered them both at home, as the Peisistradid Scythian mounted archers' corps of mercenaries in the army, to be depicted on pottery from about 530–490, and abroad, with their Black Sea colonies in the fifth and fourth centuries BC.[12]

The Greek interest in horse-breeding and riding becomes explicit in the fourth century in the works of Aristotle (384–322 BC), writing as a naturalist, and above all Xenophon (428–354), as a practical master of equitation. He had earned fame as the commander of the Greek mercenary force under the Persian king Cyrus and the heroic circumstances of the return of the Ten Thousand recounted in the *Anabasis*. About 380 he wrote his *Peri hippikes*, the Art of Equitation,[13] as a manual for the young Athenian seeking instruction in the arts of a gentleman, and it remained in its essentials a basic text for more than a thousand years of practice in western Europe, through, as we shall see, the Roman Vegetius about AD 390 and the Carolingian Rabanus Maurus about 850. The maxims of Xenophon remained sound into the Middle Ages because the technique of horse-riding had not changed over the centuries: throughout, the animal had been ridden bareback except for a horse-cloth at most, and without stirrups. The circumstances attendant on this we will discuss later in this chapter.

Westwards, wild stock of Bökönyi's Western group was available to the Roman world as well as the Eastern horses, and the riding of both was established in High Barbarian Europe by at least the sixth century. A well-known depiction in the bronze repoussé 'Situla Art' of this period from Vače, in Slovena 'illustrates a helmeted Illyrian, at home around Vače, confronting an intruder of Thracian appearance proper even to the style and bridling of his horse', the Illyrian's mount being of Western, the Thracian's of Eastern, stock.[14] 'The conscious horse-breeding of the Romans developed through the intermediary of the Greeks' from the beginning of Imperial times, and the writers on farming affairs such as Varro (*Rerum rusticarum libri III, c.*37 BC) and later Columella (*De re rustica*, AD 60–65) are concerned with breeding. Later still Vegetius in his *De re militari* of AD 383–395 deals with cavalry training in the manner of Xenophon. Looking for good breeding stock, Varro points to the Peloponnese, Thessaly and Apulia (Eastern-group horses) and Vegetius to Epirus, Dalmatia, Persia and Armenia in the ancient world of long-established breeding traditions, and again to North Africa and Spain, where as we saw in the previous chapter, good charioteering stock was likely to have been introduced in the orientalizing phase of the western Mediterranean in the eighth century BC (to be amplified in the early Middle Ages by the Arab incursions into North Africa in AD 641–687 and again into Spain in 711–732). Tacitus in the first century BC writes of the heavy demands made by Rome on horses from Gaul. For cavalry in the army, a large strong breed was achieved, standing some 145–155 cm high, as represented by the famous equestrian statue of Marcus Aurelius in Rome, to which we will return.[15]

From classical to medieval

The proud status of the horse as the unquestioned steed of prestige, the undisputed bearer of emperor and king, 'princes, magnates and knights...separated from lesser people' in western Christendom, found its origin in the Imperial Roman army. 'In Roman warfare the essential function of horses...was to serve as mounts for the emperor and his entourage when they took the field, for generals, and especially, of course, for allied and auxiliary units of cavalrymen.'[16] The Emperor was the apotheosis of the War Leader, the embodiment of victory in battle, the heroic and invincible commander in the subjugation of his enemies, and the horse, as the motive power that literally elevated him above other men, became a part of the mystique of kingship. With the ever latent anthropomorphism of antiquity, the horse became a Noble Animal, endowed with the human attributes of its rider, and by its intimate association with him, took on the qualities of a pet – a large glossy pet, expensive to acquire and costly to maintain – and as a favoured and intimate member of the family be given a name, as were the Mycenaean oxen mentioned in Chapter I, and in the same terms. Royal horses were renowned by name: the Urartian king Menua (*c.*810–786 BC) set up a surviving inscription to commemorate his horse Arsibi for making a record jump of over 11 m. Alexander's horse Bucephalus died, it is said, at 30 in the Indian campaign; the emperor Hadrian had a favourite horse named, perhaps significantly for his origins, Borysthenes (the river Dnieper), to whom an inscribed tomb was erected, recording his prowess in hunting Pannonian wild boars.[17] In the *Iliad* individual horses have colour-names (Grey, Chestnut, Bright) or attributes (Lightfoot), like the Mycenaean bovids.[18] The names of Roman chariot horses racing in the public displays have been recorded in their hundreds.

All horse-riding, from its inception until Roman times and into the earlier Middle Ages, was performed without rigid saddles or stirrups, bareback, or with one or more layers of horse-cloths or shabracks. (I use this convenient technical cavalry term 'shabrack' for a decorative parade horse-cloth, a word internationally adopted from oriental sources by the nineteenth century.) The Roman cavalry however adopted a soft thin leather (goatskin) saddle without frame but with a pair of bronze-stiffened 'horns' at front and back,[19] although the shabrack (*ephippium*) was normal and can be seen on many equestrian figures such as the Marcus Aurelius statue just

74

mentioned. Already by the fifth century BC on the steppes, at Pazyryk in the Altai, the soft shabracks were being stiffened by wooden bows, and in the later Roman Empire the texts suggest a move towards a rigid leather saddle in the *scordiscus* of Diocletian's Edict of AD 301 and the *sella* of the Theodosian Code of 438.[20] In China, rigid saddles appear from the early fourth century AD and saddle-bow plaques occur in the fourth- to sixth-century tombs of the Silla dynasty in Korea. Again in China in the mid fourth century are tomb reliefs showing types 'like the modern English saddle', and there are Hun saddles from the fifth century. In western Europe the rigid saddle had arrived to be depicted in manuscripts such as the Utrecht Psalter of c.830, or in the eleventh century on the Bayeux Tapestry.[21]

Bareback riding demanded its own set of skills, not least in orderly mounting and dismounting. Xenophon makes this clear: the seventh section of his *On Equitation* describes 'How the rider, when the horse is brought to him to mount, may conduct himself with the greatest advantage in his horsemanship both to himself and to the horse', and goes on to give in detail the essential preliminary of 'leaping' or 'jumping' on to your steed. 'And when he lightens himself for the spring up, let him pull up his body with his left hand, and keeping his right hand straight use it to help in raising himself', with further details which will concern us in a later section. This basic instruction in the leaping mount continued to be given and followed as long as harnessing remained unchanged. At the end of Roman Imperial times, about AD 383–395, Vegetius in his military handbook, *Epitoma rei militaris*, enlarged on training for the leaping mount with wooden vaulting 'horses' in a gymnasium, and an abridgement of his book, discarding what was seen as irrelevant to modern practice, was made in the ninth century AD by Rabanus Maurus, a remarkable man who was a pupil of Alcuin, a distinguished poet; he ended his life as Archbishop of Mainz 847–856. A favourite of Lothair I (823–855), Rabanus must have been well acquainted with contemporary horsemanship in the 850s when he wrote. He repeats Vegetius on the leaping mount and the use of wooden horses for practice, and adds that this manner of mounting and 'exercise of jumping has flourished greatly among the Frankish people'.[22] Conservative harnessing techniques over the centuries, like the yoke and the breast-strap in traction, led to a continuity in instruction from Xenophon to Vegetius of over 750 years; from Vegetius to Rabanus another 450 or so – a total of over a millennium of jumping on and off horses. Change was only to come, as we shall see, by

9 *Rubbing of Han Dynasty relief from China with a rider without stirrups or rigid saddle.*

innovative harnessing with stirrups and rigid saddles, in the western world of the later ninth century AD. We move from the Old Horsemanship of classical antiquity to the New Horsemanship of the Middle Ages.

Display and majesty

Before we leave the Roman world we may briefly touch on two themes proper to our pursuit of the horse as a symbol of prestige, horsemanship as display and as a part of the embodiment of Imperial majesty. In the Roman cavalry there grew up a tradition of sports or exercises in peace time, known to Arrian, writing in Greek in AD 136, as the *hippika gymnasia*, which were complex displays of horsemanship combining the features of an elaborate circus act and the eighteenth-century Haute École. Behind them, as Jocelyn Toynbee pointed out, must lie the ancient, traditional, legendary and part-mythical rite, the *lusus Troiae*, the Trojan Game, 'highly intricate riding exercises carried out by youths and boys of noble birth who rode in labyrinthine formation in two or three separate bands...wheeling, attacking, separating and joining up again in a mock fight,' as described by Virgil and many other writers. Arrian gives a long and vivid account of the cavalry games which, on account of the foreign technical terms he had to translate, made him look to Celtic or perhaps Iberian origins for the show: we may recall the Indo-Aryan words in Kikulli, the Mitannian's horse-training manual, of the second millennium BC quoted in the last chapter. The games were performed by those of 'conspicuous rank or for skill in horsemanship' wearing helmets with face-vizors and yellow plumes 'which make a brave show, waving in the air under the influence of the breeze'; they carried light oblong gaily painted shields. 'Instead of breast-plates they wear tunics...sometimes scarlet, sometimes purple, sometimes particoloured. And they have trousers not loose like those in fashion among the Persians and Armenians, but closely fitting to the limbs.' Their horses wore decorated shabracks (*ephippia*) and chamfrons, and they carried light lances, some bearing 'Scythian pennants made of brightly coloured cloth stitched together in the form of a serpent'. Horses and riders performed complex feats of equitation, throwing lances in mock combat.[23]

Whatever the origins of the Trojan Game or the army's cavalry sports, they are, with their plumes and pennons, disguising and masking, and brightly coloured exotic clothes, very uncharacteristic of the classical Roman ethos with its sober restraint and professional pursuit of good order and military discipline. The *lusus*, widely thought of as venerably ancient at the time, might well go back to a prehistoric Italian past; Arrian recognized the sports he described as barbarian and extraneous, perhaps Celtic. Something of barbarian feats of ostentatious virtuosity in horsemanship can be glimpsed after the end of the Empire in the sixth century AD. The army of the emperor Justinian in Italy under Narses confronted and eventually defeated the Ostrogoths under their king, Totila, in AD 552. The armies were arrayed and each exhorted his troops. Expecting reinforcements and playing for time, Totila staged a delaying action by feats of personal equestrian display.

First of all, he was not reluctant to make an exhibition to the enemy of what manner of man he was. For the armour in which he was clad was abundantly plated with gold and the ample adornments which hung from his cheek-plates as well as from his helmet and spear were not only of purple but in other respects resembling a king, marvellous in their abundance. And he himself, sitting on a very large horse, began to perform the dance under arms skilfully between the armies. For he wheeled his horse round in a circle and then turned him again to the other side and so made him run round and round. And as he rode he hurled his javelin into the air and caught it again as it quivered above him, then passed it rapidly from hand to hand, shifting it with consummate skill, and he gloried in his practice in such matters, falling back on his shoulders, spreading his legs and leaning from side to side, like one who has been instructed in the art of dancing from childhood.[24]

This panache was appropriate enough to a barbarian king but hardly suitable for an emperor or patrician representative of a constitution devoted to proclaiming itself as the embodiment of civilized power. The emperor in official art, with its high propaganda content, would, if shown on horseback, be the portrayal of a high-ranking cavalry general on a dignified standing or pacing steed. The latter became an artistic convention in which the horse, with one foreleg raised, was adopted on coins, sculpture and equestrian statues and became not only the standard Roman schema, itself adopted from Hellenistic models, but continued through the Middle Ages and the Renaissance to the nineteenth century, to be used as the traditional portrayal of the monarch. The most influential single piece in antiquity was perhaps the famous equestrian statue of Marcus Aurelius, emperor AD 161–180, and it is worthwhile *pl. 6* considering it in more detail. This superb piece of gilded bronze is recorded in the tenth century as standing in the Piazza del Laterano in Rome, where it was preserved with veneration by the Christian authorities in the pious belief that it represented the emperor Constantine. In 1538 it was moved to the Piazza del Campidoglio to stand on a pedestal designed by Michelangelo, but had to be removed in 1981 for conservation.[25] Marcus Aurelius is of course shown riding without stirrups and on an elaborate four-layered shabrack with dentated edges, and the raised right hoof of the horse seems originally to have rested on a small crouching barbarian figure. This pose, symbolic of the conquest of the lesser breeds without the law, was frequent in Imperial Roman official art in sculpture and as a coin type, but the pacing horse with lifted foot alone was what was to enter the stock vocabulary of artistic images. Apart from contemporary classical versions, already in the Romano-Celtic Gaul of the second century AD is the fine bronze figure of a pacing horse, 1.05 m high, from the native sanctuary site at Neuvy-en-Sullias on the Loire near Orléans, and small bronze votive horses in the same pose come from Roman Britain.[26] The pacing horse in the well-known little statuette of the ninth century reputedly of Charlemagne, formerly in the Cathedral of Metz and now in the Musée Carnavalet, must be taken with caution as it was heavily restored in 1507, but its stance is likely to have remained unchanged.[27]

The egregious forgery of the so-called Donation of Constantine, fabricated in the papal chancery of Pope Stephen II (752–757) and attributed to the emperor Constantine, allegedly conferred or confirmed the papacy in territorial and imperial rights, so that the pope, as a monarch, would properly be mounted on an appropriate steed. In a fresco of 1246 in the church of SS Quattro Cornati in Rome, Constantine is shown making his 'donation' to Pope Sylvester I, which includes a white horse with raised front hoof: here the Constantine attribution could link statue and steed. Thereafter in the Renaissance popes ride like monarchs on white pacing horses.[28] From the beginning of the fifteenth century there follow such famous equestrian statues of noblemen as those by Donatello and Verrochio, and the statues of European monarchs up to the well-known Charles I of England by Le Sueur (1630; set up at Charing Cross 1674) or Louis XIV of France by Giradon in Paris, of 1695. The heroized monarch on horseback as icon and symbol remained constant from Marcus Aurelius until the eve of modern times.

1,2 The Royal Lion Hunt on reliefs of Assurbanipal (669–626 BC), Mesopotamia.

OPPOSITE
3–5 (*Above*) Dismembered chariots in the tomb of Tutankhamun at Thebes, mid fourteenth century BC. (*Centre*) Tutankhamun's Royal Lion Hunt, painted on a box from his tomb. (*Below*) Stone stele with chariot warrior, Mycenae Shaft Graves, seventeenth century BC.

6–8 (*Above*) Equestrian statue of Marcus Aurelius, Roman emperor AD 161–180, standing on its plinth designed by Michelangelo. (*Below left*) Gallo-Roman relief of the goddess Epona riding side-saddle. (*Below*) Rider with flounced tunic and trousers, on a silver helmet from Agighiol, Romania, about 375–340 BC.

HAROLD REX INTERFEC TVS EST

9–12 (*Above*) Stripping the dead of their mail shirts after the battle of Hastings, 1066, shown on the Bayeux Tapestry. (*Left*) Roman cavalrymen riding down the natives, on a relief slab commemorating the beginning of the building of the Antonine Wall in AD 142, from Bridgeness, Scotland. (*Opposite above*) The carriage from Pazyryk in the Altai, fifth century BC. (*Opposite below*) Reconstructed carriage from the Hochdorf tomb, Hallstatt D, about 500 BC.

13–15 (*Above*) Pleasure carriage with noble ladies, from the Luttrell Psalter, about AD 1320–40. (*Below*) Model of Queen Elizabeth's presentation coach to the Tsar Boris Godunov, 1603. (*Opposite below*) The Boris Godunov coach open, showing the 'side-saddle' steps for the lady attendant.

16,17 (*Above*) The Royal Gold State Coach of George III, 1762. (*Below*) The Lord Mayor of London's Coach, 1757.

From the Old Horsemanship to the New

The Old Horsemanship of western Europe, with its athletic requirements for mounting and the subsequent management of a horse
ridden bareback, continued in antiquity until the adoption of three
technological innovations: stirrups, a rigidly framed saddle, and iron
shoes nailed to the horse's hoofs (this last of lesser importance in
warfare, but of universal application in horse-driving as well as
riding). The introduction of the first of these new devices, the rigid
stirrup to take the motion from and to support the rider's feet, has
provoked a degree of historical controversy which in the perspective
of archaeology and ancient horse management today seems excessive.
In its original form in the early 1960s, the dispute involved not only
the history of warfare and the military consequences deciding the
fate of the European nations in the eighth century AD, but also the
legal and constitutional problems of the inception of western medieval
feudalism in the same period. These are not topics of concern to us
here in the pursuit of the mounting of the nobility and gentry, nor
do they seem today so inevitably linked to the use of stirrups as
appeared to the earlier protagonists, and the issues have now shifted
in emphasis. What emerges from the great stirrup controversy seems
to be as follows.[29]

Experiments in horse harness to increase the stability and control
of the rider were taking place in the Orient with simple rope loops
or metal hook-stirrups from the late centuries BC, appearing in India
(toe-loops) and Scythian and Kushan contexts (hooks). The rigid
wood- or metal-framed stirrup is present in China and Korea around
the fourth to sixth centuries AD, and the iron pear-shaped form
ancestral to medieval European types appears in Japan *c.*AD 470–550
and first in Europe in seventh-century Avar graves in Hungary. In
the west, stirrups first appear shown in a St Gall manuscript of
*c.*863–883, and archaeological and literary sources suggest that 'the
stirrup was little appreciated and little used by the Carolingians
during the eighth and ninth centuries' but was established by the
tenth. Its use was not dependent on the rigid wood-framed saddle
and it developed without it in the Orient, but in the west the two
in combination enabled the military technique of shock combat,
with the couched heavy lance rigidly and horizontally held, to be
developed, but hardly before the twelfth century. As we saw, suitable
saddles were being developed in the west by the ninth century, as
were horseshoes, first mentioned in the second half of the century

in the poem *Waltharius* and known from actual ninth-to-tenth-century finds in England. Horseshoes of the late pre-Roman Iron Age have been claimed from Austria, and such continuity in the smith's craft from prehistory into history might not be impossible when one remembers the shrunk-on hoop tyre and perhaps animal-headed fire-dogs.[30] Whatever criticisms of Professor Lynn White's original stirrup thesis may be levelled, his wider contention of the innovative quality of early medieval technology remains valid and valuable and he has expressed the view that 'the vigor of medieval technology may have been simply an amplification of a cultural condition preexistent in Gaul'.[31] There is much to be said for this idea, and here we may be seeing it expressed in the ready adoption of new ideas from the Orient together with developments from older local equine traditions to form the combination of efficient management and control that marked the New Horsemanship from the end of the ninth century AD.

Work-horse and pack-horse

Lower in the social scale than the Noble Horse (increasingly referred to as the Great Horse (*magnus equus*), where the adjective is as much one of status as of stature, still around the 150 cm range), there developed in western Europe, beyond or overlapping with the Mediterranean donkey and mule zone, the working horse on farms and roads.[32] Excluding for the moment draught (it too rendered a New Horsemanship by the adoption of harness with shafts and rigid collars from the ninth century; whipple-trees and tandem draught by the twelfth), an important transport facility was that afforded by pack animals. In northwest Europe the pack horse took over from donkeys and mules during the early Middle Ages and continued until modern times. Small, sturdy, reliable and strong, the pack animal's load in classical times has been estimated at 150 kg for mules, and 99–150 kg for the medieval horse.[33] For the conductors of the pack train on an ambling or pacing pony the refinements of stirrups may have meant little, but from the rigid-framed pack saddle of the load-bearing beasts came a riding device of considerable significance for the west, the side-saddle for women.

Women on horseback

One of the best-known examples of a caravan trade with pack donkeys in the ancient Near East is that of the early second millennium BC between Assyria and the Anatolian trading-city of Kanesh (Kültepe); textiles and tin ingots were involved, and the latter have a particular importance in the vexed question of tin sources in antiquity. A sealing from Kültepe of this period shows a figure on an equid 'seated sideways on what seems a rigid-framed pack saddle to which a low back rest and a footrest have been attached',[34] and by the middle of the millennium in Egypt the Deir-el-Bahri reliefs of Queen Hatshepsut's expedition to Punt (on the Somali coast) show the portly queen of Punt, Eti, riding side-saddle on a donkey; petroglyphs in Sinai show robed personages similarly mounted. Coming down to classical times in the west the Gallo-Roman horse goddess Epona is always depicted as riding side-saddle *pl. 7* and Vigneron commenting on this suggests a derivation of the woman's saddle from the framed pack saddle.[35] The wooden frame of a pack saddle of the late pre-Roman Iron Age actually survives from La Tène in Switzerland.[36] In the Middle Ages depictions of women on side-saddles occur, and so on into the seventeenth century (as in Loggan's Cambridge views of 1675), but all are in saddles of the chair-set-sideways type, never with stirrups, which seem to have been used in the modern manner of side-saddle riding sporadically from fifteenth-century France, and increasingly in the nineteenth century.[37]

In the east the story is quite different, where women rode astride their horses from at least the fifth century BC: unlike their western sisters they habitually wore not long skirts but trousers as part of a tradition of costume which has divided Europe from much of Asia until today. A Persian miniature painting of the sixteenth century, for instance, shows a polo match between two teams of jolly trousered girls astride their elegant horses, and earlier in the west Herodotus in the fifth century BC (IV, 116) reported that the Sarmatian women of the lower Volga steppes 'observe their ancient customs, frequently hunting on horseback with their husbands . . . in war taking to the field; and wearing the very same dress as the men'. Sarmatian graves of the period have women buried with archer's equipment: Greek myth turned these frightening women into Amazons. The timid Edward Gibbon was clearly lost in admiration for the masterful Zenobia, Queen of Palmyra from AD 267 – 'perhaps the only female whose superior genius broke through the servile indolence imposed on her sex by the climate and manners of Asia', who 'disdained the use of a covered carriage' and 'generally appeared on horseback in a military habit'.[38] But you never could tell with those oriental queens: in the early third century BC Ptolemy's queen Arsinoe was said to have ridden an ostrich.[39]

Riding and clothing: Greeks and barbarians

The contrast between the dress of women riders in the eastern and western worlds of horsemanship touches on a subject which though of some interest in cultural history seems not to have been discussed as a whole: the interaction between horseriding and the clothing of men and women who rode, at all levels of the social scale from monarch to peasant. I therefore propose making a digression which may point to some tentative conclusions between about 600 BC and AD 1000, a period of good documentation over a millennium and a half for the changes in European costume from ancient to modern, on horseback or on foot. Male clothing undergoes the greatest change, women's dress is more conservative, perhaps because in the west men rode horses in hunting, on business, for sport or for war, as well as on occasions of pomp and the display of authority, and it was riding that promoted the modifications in sartorial fashions. As we shall see, our essential quest is the history of trousers in antiquity.

When, twenty-five years ago, I made a brief comment on Eurasiatic dress in prehistory, I proposed a broad division between 'the tailored garments normally consisting of trousers and coat, and the single-piece wrapped style': before me, in the instance of Scythian clothing, Ellis Minns had commented on its 'coats and trousers...tailor's work as against the sheets and plaids worn by Europe and fastened by pins and clasps'. The tailored garment in skin or fur has great antiquity in the north. Upper Palaeolithic human figurines from sites on the Angara River show people clad in fur trousers and tunic, and such clothing has persisted to the present day among circumpolar groups such as the Eskimos: *anorak*, the name of the upper garment, has become almost the only loan-word (with *kayak*) from Inuit in the English language.[40] The single-piece sheet of textile gives a simple and adaptable garment – the sarong or burnous at one end of the climatic scale, the male skirts of Bronze Age Denmark, or the Scottish plaid (before the invention of the kilt in its modern form about 1740), on the other. As a single-piece outer garment the cloak, of varying length, is of course universal and obvious.

When I wrote (in *Ancient Europe*) I did not appreciate the importance of a simple intermediate garment, the tubular sleeved tunic: Greek *chiton*, Latin *tunica*. This was the essential male garment for riding a horse in Europe from at least the sixth century BC until the early Middle Ages: usually short-sleeved, it was worn over bare legs in the classical world where it could vary from ankle to calf length, and obviously for riding a short tunic was appropriate. In classical Greece the long chiton, full, belted and ankle-length, is worn by the famous bronze of the standing charioteer from Delphi of about 475 BC; the short horse-rider's version, closer fitting but with a flaring pleated or flounced thigh-length skirt, is seen on many vase-paintings and on two well-known pieces of sculpture, the stele of Dixileos who fell in the Corinthian War in 394, and the Bryaxis relief of 340–330.[41] This type of chiton was worn by the barbarians outside Greece as we shall see shortly and was directly ancestral to the tunic of the Roman army and hence of the highest rank, in whose uniform the Roman emperor paraded in his capacity of tutelary warrior. Throughout it was worn over bare legs, and here we should look back for a moment to Xenophon and his instructions for mounting by jumping on to the horse. After the passage quoted earlier on the rider using his right hand 'to help in raising himself' he goes on, 'If he mounts in this way he will not provide an unseemly spectacle from behind by bending his leg . . . and when he has brought his foot over, then let him lower his buttocks on to the horse.' Despite the Greek predilection for nude young athletes, while these were admissible riding bareback, decorum decreed that when clothed in a chiton, they should not in mounting display a bare backside. Hence too the value of the shabrack: in Rome the poet Martial later characteristically wrote, 'Mounting bareback can give you piles'.[42]

The engraved and repoussé bronzes in the 'Situla Style' have already been referred to in connection with their depiction of horse types round the head of the Adriatic in the sixth century BC, and the two confronted riders from Vače both wear close-fitted tunics with wide flared thigh-length skirts over bare legs in the manner of the Greek chiton. Such garments are shown worn by horsemen on other pieces, flounced or fringed, and on one situla (Arnoaldi) foot soldiers with long 'Celtic' shields wear fringed tunics.[43] But when we turn to other tunic-wearing riders in contemporary Europe we encounter a novelty: tight trousers worn under the skirted chiton. Now for the Greeks, as later the Romans, trousers were the sure sign of the outsider and barbarian, and with the self-righteous Puritan streak in Greek xenophobia trousers, together with the use of colours and embroidery in clothing, carried with them the stigma of oriental effeminacy, luxury

and despotism (perhaps unconsciously reflecting Greek technical inferiority in weaving and dye-stuffs). Lexically, the Greek for trousers is a loan-word, *anaxurides*, used for instance by Herodotus and Xenophon of Scythians and Persians and said to derive from the latter language. Euripides and Aristophanes call the loose Persian trousers *thulakoi*, 'bags', and perhaps a donnish joke introduced the word to English slang in the 1860s – from Persian Bags to Oxford Bags. When about 530–490 BC a mercenary corps of mounted Scythian archers was formed in Athens, they immediately caught the fancy of the vase-painters, who drew these exotic figures in tight flounced or simple tunics and tight trousers in gaily sprigged or patterned fabrics: there seems to have been a change in Scythian fashion by the later fourth century, when the well-known Graeco-Scythian silver and gold work shows looser trousers than the earlier paintings.[44] But in the

10 *Celtic horsemen wearing flounced tunics and trousers, on an engraved
scabbard of the fifth century* BC *from Hallstatt, Austria.*

lower Danube adjacent to Scythian territory on its east an indigenous
style of decorated silver, silver-gilt and gold work from tombs and
hoards of *c.*375–340 BC depicts horsemen (on for instance the Agighiol   *pl. 8*
silver helmet and the Letnitsa gold plaques)[45] with full-skirted tunic
and tight trousers once again. And from the well-known Austrian
site of Hallstatt comes an engraved sword-scabbard of early Celtic
date, late fifth to early fourth century BC, with once more horsemen
in flounced tunics and horizontally striped tight trousers.[46] From the
Scythians on the Black Sea to the Celts of central Europe a consistent
pattern of horseman's wear, tight trousers under flounced tunic, was
clearly well established from at least 500 BC. Away on the fringe of
the Scythian world in Central Asia of the fifth century BC, from one
of the Pazyryk tombs in the Altai, comes a coloured felt hanging
showing a dashing horseman with curled moustaches and flying blue

spotted red cloak, in a tight wrap-over blue tunic with embroidered edges and flared skirt, over brown tights.[47] The famous Gundestrup cauldron, found dismembered in a bog in Denmark, is now to be seen as a piece of Thracian silver-work of the early second century BC, probably made by local Danubian craftsmen for Celtic patrons, and perhaps looted and carried back to the north by the Cimbri in 118 BC. One plaque shows riders and foot-soldiers, the former ride bare-legged with short ribbed and skirted tunics, helmets and laced shoes with spurs; the others have close-fitting ribbed tunics, broad belts and tight knee-length breeches. The costumes depicted seem unique.

Rome and after

What we have been seeing of course are the exotic riders in Arrian's cavalry games, and this takes us back to Imperial Rome and what was normal, not odd, in the cavalryman's clothing which was also that of the emperor in his equestrian rôle. This was the standard legionary wear which, under any armour that might be worn, was precisely the Greek chiton with thigh-length flared skirt over bare legs, seen on innumerable sculptures, including portrait statues of emperors.[48] The tunic would have presented the same problems of decorum in mounting by jumping on the horse as described by Xenophon and his successors. Documentary and pictorial sources are, not surprisingly, reticent on the subject of underpants, but leather briefs worn under the tunic were standard legionary issue and can often be detected on sculpture (as for instance on Trajan's Column) and on auxiliaries could amount to knee-length breeches.

In his masterly review of Roman provincial clothing in the northwest of the Empire,[49] J.P. Wild wrote, 'Beyond the bounds of the Empire to the North and East, from the Danube to the Black Sea, stretched a band of barbari whose main garb, regardless of nationality, was in essence long-sleeved tunic, cloak and trousers', but the iconographic evidence from Gaul and Britain shows tunic and cloak alone: perhaps as Wild suggests we are relying mainly on sculptured tomb-slabs to prosperous citizens, eager to be up-and-coming in the new Roman world and so avoiding the taint of barbarism. For 'the Romans of Rome affected a thorough-going snobbery to trousers, which were before the late second century AD considered only fit for barbarians to wear'; the wearing of them within the city of Rome was forbidden by an edict of the emperor

Honorius (AD 393–423). Trousered barbarians became a literary and artistic topos in classical times, whether Celts or Germans, Scythians or Parthians: a series of genre sculptures of the 'Dying Barbarian' are either naked or trousered.[50] For the garments, Latin used a loan-word, Celtic with a Germanic root, *bracae* (English 'breeches'). Transalpine Gaul was *Gallia bracata* when it was not *comata*, long-haired and equally disparaging. A monument from the city of Volubilis in North Africa shows how a Roman artist rendered barbarians he could never have seen. The bronze statue on which they are engraved is from a monument to the emperor M. Aurelius Antoninus (Caracalla) about AD 210–217, and shows the conventional scene of two captives flanking a trophy of armour. The inscription described Caracalla as *Parthicus maximus* and *Britannicus maximus*, commemorating his victories in Parthia and North Britain, and both captives are trousered, one in the curious slashed and buttoned garments known for instance from sculpture at Hatra, and the other in *bracae* of loud and disparate checks.[51]

We are brought back once again to Arrian. When he describes the exotic clothes of the cavalry performers he says that their trousers are 'not loose like those in fashion among the Parthians and Armenians, but fitting closely to the limbs'. This must be a reminiscence or quotation from Tacitus's account of the Germans, written nearly forty years earlier in AD 98, where he states 'the wealthiest are distinguished by a dress which is not flowing like that of the Sarmatians and Parthians but is tight and exhibits each limb' (*Germ.* XVII); such clothing is shown on captives on the Trajan and Antonine columns, and actual trousers of the Roman Iron Age have been found in North German bogs such as Thorsberg, Damdorf and Daetgen Mose.[52] Suitable horseman's clothes for riders north of the Alps, with a prehistory going back to the fifth century BC, were now in a position to take their place among the barbarians who themselves were to create a new medieval civilization on the ruins of the classical world. The baggy trousers of the Orient were replaced by more closely tailored garments in the northwest, and with the short tunic formed admirable riding clothes in cold or wet weather, replacing the skirted tunic worn bare-legged south of the Alps for horsemen from emperor to peasant: we shall see actual Emperor's New Clothes when we move for instance from the equestrian portrayal of Marcus Aurelius the Imperial Roman to a description of Charlemagne, crowned Holy Roman Emperor on Christmas Day AD 800, and his Frankish court.

The Franks came from north Germany and the shores of the Baltic, tribes adjacent to and contemporary in their migrations with the Angles, Saxons and Jutes who invaded late Roman Britain. Franks were moving south into Gaul from the early fifth century and from 486 under their king Clovis, baptized a Christian some time after 493 at Rheims, became the rulers of Gaul, *regnum Francorum*, a state with strong Roman ties. Clovis consolidated the Merovingian dynasty, the last members of which we met in their ox-carriages in Chapter I, and in 719 a palace revolution under Charles Martel introduced a new line of which Charlemagne (768–814) was the most distinguished member, and the personal instigator and patron of a notable revival in art and letters.

One product of the Carolingian renaissance was the writing, about 880, of a book of gossipy reminiscences of the emperor by a monk of St Gall, almost certainly Notker nicknamed the Stammerer.[53] More diffuse and less reliable than Einhard's Suetonian biography, it nevertheless contains a wealth of fascinating detail, not least a full account of the traditional clothing of the king and court. One anecdote of Charlemagne leading to another 'brings me now to his clothing in time of war. The dress and equipment of the Old Franks was as follows', writes Notker. Gilded boots were 'decorated with leather laces more than four feet long', 'the wrapping round their legs were scarlet'. Such simple one-piece leggings are shown on a Gallo-Roman relief at Neumagen and survive as bog finds from Hanover and Denmark.[54] Notker goes on, 'Under these they wore linen garments on their legs and thighs, of the same colour, but with elaborate embroidery. Long leather thongs were cross-gartered over these wrappings and linen garments, in and out, in front and behind.' These were presumably the four-foot long bootlaces with which he started, and he goes on, 'Next came a white linen shirt, round which was buckled a sword-belt . . . the last item of their clothing was a cloak, either white or blue, in the shape of a double square.' Here at the close of the ninth century we have the emperor clothed no longer in the Roman manner but that of the new world of the western Middle Ages; a long-haired Frank not only in trousers but in scarlet embroidered ones, the embodiment of barbarity to the austere short-back-and-sides, tunic-clad figure of the Augustan age. It is interesting to see how the monk of St Gall had trouble with his Latin vocabulary for the non-classical clothes: for the shirt or tunic he uses *camisia* (French 'chemise') first used in Latin in the late fourth century by St Jerome, who apologizes for it as *sermo vulgatus*, and a loan-word with Germanic roots.[55] For trousers, Notker gives up and resorts to a periphrasis not unlike Tacitus, though he could have used *bracae*, with the same Germano-Celtic origins as *camisia*.

By the ninth century AD we see current in western Europe the horseman's clothes of tunic and close-fitting trousers or breeches established at least from the fifth century BC among barbarian Scythians, Dacians or Celts; the classical world has been sartorially rejected. The pattern was now set for modern Europe; with the adoption of buttoned garments from about 1300,[56] the tunic became the coat, and with close-fitting trousers was ancestral to the western business suit. The Orient retained the loose trousers for both sexes – *pyjamas*, entering the English language from Urdu through India about 1800, the English bed about a century later. But eastern modes continued to affect Europe, for when in 1666 Charles II set a new fashion at court it was for 'the Eastern fashion of vest…a comely vest after the Persian mode' as John Evelyn put it, and who was so impressed by 'the comelinesse and usefulness of the Persian clothing' that he wrote a pamphlet in its praise.[57] The long buttoned coat indeed goes back in Persia to Achaemenid times, and was eventually the ancestor of that emblem of upper class respectability, the Victorian frock coat.

Stranger still in the history of the interaction of riding and clothing is the American phenomenon. With the first introduction of horsemanship to the New World from Spain in the sixteenth century, tight trousers became the working wear of the cattle rancher, and when in modern years the extraordinary cult of the mythical nineteenth-century American West was linked with a naive inverted snobbery, the cotton trousers of the cowboy were elevated to the worldwide symbol of western democracy as blue jeans.

Knights in armour: from prehistory into history

We may finally take a brief look at a special type of clothing for the privileged horseman in antiquity, the industrial protective clothing of the warrior and the heavy-duty overalls in that ancient industry, warfare: armour for rider and horse. Apart from its rôle in enhancing prestige while being highly functional, the early development of armour nicely illustrates two of the main themes in this book – the continuity between the prehistoric and the early historical evidence, and the interaction between Europe and Western Asia over a couple of millennia. Throughout, armour is not only protective and prestigious, but it is technologically demanding and proportionately expensive, and a bronze corselet or a shirt of iron mail as valuable a perquisite as a good sword, whether acquired from an armourer or looted in battle. Addressing the Classical Association some years ago, General Sir John Hackett, as a soldier and its President, stressed that all ancient engagements in the field were in modern terms 'recovery battles' and instanced the systematic stripping of the dead of their arms in Homer: 'the importance of weapons, of their possession, retention, loss and retrieval is in the *Iliad* everywhere apparent'.[58] Even if 'in no single passage of the *Iliad* or *Odyssey* can we be certain whether the poet is describing, accurately or otherwise, the arms and practices of that earlier [Mycenaean] period or those of his own day',[59] the practice was common to all early warfare. Eighteen hundred years or so later than the Homeric redaction, the Bayeux Tapestry shows in its lower register below the final episodes of the Battle of Hastings, lively scenes of those scavenging on the *pl. 9* battlefield for swords and shields, while systematically stripping the dead of their shirts of mail.[60]

The body armour we have to consider falls into two groups; sheet metal corselets (which from the naturalistic modelling of the pectoral muscles in many Greek and Roman examples has led to the term 'muscle cuirasses'), and the various types of tunic armoured with small plates, scales or interlocked rings constituting shirts of lamellar or scale armour or of mail ('chain mail' is an otiose form not used by historians of armour). The bronze corselet in its final form as seen in Imperial Roman portrayals of emperors or high ranking military officers has a curious history, for behind its classical appearance from Greek hoplite to Roman emperor lie origins in the world contemptuously designated (it could hardly be dismissed) as barbarian Europe. Anthony Snodgrass has traced the early story of European body-armour with conviction.[61]

Northwards of the limited areas of early Greece and Rome in the Aegean and the central Mediterranean from the end of the second millennium BC lay the prehistoric cultures of the High Bronze Age and from the end of the eighth century BC, the earlier Iron Age (Urnfields and Hallstatt to the archaeologist). By about 1200 BC, at least three finds in Slovakia show that sheet bronze corselets, of a type to continue for some centuries, were being made by Central European armourers, and, presumably as a result of their first western trade and colonies (before 750 BC at Pithekoussai and Cumae), the Greeks encountered this fine tradition of body armour, and adopted it, as the bronze corselet of Central European derivation from a warrior's grave of about 725 BC at Argos testifies. This is the direct ancestor of the later hoplite body armour up to the fifth century, whence from Hellenistic sources it was taken up by Republican Rome; in Imperial times such body armour remained the 'symbol of Roman might and sovereignty...the recognized distinction of the military leader' to the fourth and even the fifth century AD.[62]

But it was not plate corselets (if we continue this odd zigzag history from west to east and back again) that were to prevail in early medieval Europe after the fall of the Empire, but rather the flexible, lighter armoured tunics of fabric and metal plates, scales or interlocking wire rings. In the northwest the last, the mail shirt, from at least the two or three centuries BC, was to dominate the scene until the Middle Ages. Here we have an ancient Near Eastern tradition once again adopted and transmitted westwards by the barbarians beyond the classical world, technologically innovative and receptive of outside influences. Various forms of lamellar and scale-armoured shirts are known from before the middle of the second millennium BC in Mesopotamia and Egypt, differing only in how the little bronze platelets were sewn on to their linen backing to overlap laterally or hang like tiles. From the Mitannian town of Nuzi southwest of Kirkuk,[63] founded before at least a dated letter in its archives of *c*.1460 BC, come not only actual finds of lamellar and scale armour, but cuneiform documents listing even the number of scales on the shirts held in the stores. Some finds and many representations in Egypt, from half-a-dozen reigns from Thutmose III about 1450 to Ramesses II at the battle of Kadesh, and even Sheshonk after 940 BC, show the enduring popularity of the lamellar and scale corselet.[64] The style was to be taken up by the Persians – Herodotus noted how they wore 'tunics with sleeves, of divers colours, having iron scales upon them like the scales of a fish' (VII.61), and contemporary or rather earlier is the bronze scale armour of the Scythians, going back to the sixth century.[65] In fourth-century Thrace, the gold plaques from Letnitsa near Lovech in Bulgaria, of about 350 BC, show horsemen wearing scale corselets over skirted chitons.[66] Westwards this oriental tradition seems to have reached Cyprus by the sixth century, but Greek usage was rare and sporadic and mainly in the Black Sea colonies in Scythian territory. In Italy itself the scales of a mail shirt are said to have come from Lake Trasimene and to be associated with Hannibal's victory of 217 BC. Scale armour (*lorica squamata*) became widespread in the Roman Imperial army, especially for auxiliaries up to the fourth century AD and beyond.[67] The wars and annexations of Dacia in AD 101–105 and those against the Marcomanni and Sarmatians in 175 brought the Roman army into regions with a long tradition of scale armour, to be represented on the Trajan and Aurelian columns; at Dura Europos on the Euphrates, northeast of Damascus, the Roman garrison was destroyed by the Sassanians in AD 256 and archaeologists have found scale armour for horses as well as the well-known graffito of an armoured knight on an armoured horse.[68] By the beginning of the fifth century AD recognized titles are given to armoured knights, *cataphractarius* and *clibanarius*: semantically both imply restricted enclosure, *clibanus* being a closed bell-shaped bread oven, very appropriate to a shirt of armour on a hot summer's campaign.

But the flexible reinforced body armour which was to prevail from non-classical antiquity, to dominate the earlier medieval world of the mounted knight, was the shirt of mail made of interlocking rings of iron wire, the true 'mail'. The classical world was well aware of it,[69] and about 43 BC Varro attributed its invention to the Gauls, among whom Diodorus Siculus, using Posidonius about 60–30 BC, said iron mail shirts were in use.[70] The Roman army used it from the first century BC to at least the third century AD, and it is frequently shown in Gaulish sculpture, from the figures in the oppidum and sanctuary of the Saluvii at Entremont, destroyed in 123 BC, onwards. Mail was found with a pre-Flavian burial at Chassemard, Auvergne, and there are several finds of late Iron Age and early Roman date from Britain. A Gallo-Roman inscription at Nevers records an armourer making mail among the Aedui.[71] All this, however, is at the end of a longer story. Shirts of mail were worn in barbarian Europe from the Black Sea to the Baltic in the later pre-Roman Iron Age by a number of peoples, beginning with the Scythians, whose inventive genius was influenced by the traditions of the ancient Orient, and whose armourers made not only lamellar and scale corselets, but mail. At least two graves near Kiev – Smela and Zhurovka – contained shirts of mail, the latter with a fifth-century BC Greek lekythos (the Sarmatians moved from scale armour to mail only in the late first century AD).[72] The tale is then taken up on the lower Danube, in the Ciumeşti tomb in Romania of the second to third century BC[73] and in central Europe at Horny Jatov in Slovakia earlier,[74] in the third or fourth century. The votive deposit of the second to third century BC at Hjortspring on the Danish island of

Als contained an estimated twenty shirts of mail.[75] And in Britain very recent finds of such mail come from second-century BC Iron Age graves in the Yorkshire Wolds.[76] At the other end of the Celtic world, the early first-century BC Galatian trophies shown on the reliefs at Pergamon in Anatolia include mail shirts of the same type.[77]

In the Germanic north beyond the bounds of the Roman Empire mail shirts have been found in warriors' graves and the votive deposits of Vimose and Thorsberg, all around the third century AD.[78] By the time of the mail in the Sutton Hoo royal burial of *c.*630 we are at the beginning of the northwestern European Middle Ages. The armoured knight on horseback and equipped with a lance, as we begin to see him in manuscripts such as the Gellone Sacramentary (790–795) or the St Gall Psalter (890–924),[79] is a figure with a long prehistoric and oriental lineage. In the east the Naqsh-i-Rustam reliefs show the Sassanian cavalry under Bahram II (AD 276–293) with couched lance and rigid saddle in the manner of much later knights in the west. Then there is Viking mail at, for instance, ninth-century Birka, and the mail shirt of St Wenceslas, AD 935, preserved in the cathedral of Prague.[80] Davis quotes the Edict of Pîtres by Charles the Bald (864) prohibiting the ransom of mail to the Vikings, and Charlemagne's son, Louis the Pious, reported in 795 his loot in Spain of a 'fine horse, a fine coat of mail and an Indian sword'.[81] The Monk of St Gall, describing Charlemagne himself in full armour at the siege of Pavia in 773, is lyrical on the sheer amount of iron *ferreus Karolus* carried on helmet, corselet, thigh armour, gloves and greaves.[82] The armourer's technology was clearly one to be proud of.

A final prehistoric contribution to the medieval armoured knight's equipment is the prick spur. Spurs are known in graves and settlements of the early Iron Age from the fifth to first centuries BC in Gaul and Central Europe, and on the riders on the Gundestrup cauldron. They were sporadically used by Roman cavalry on the Continent and Britain, especially by troops on the Rhine-Danube *limes*, and were known in Greece from the fifth century BC onwards. They reappear in Merovingian graves where, as in prehistoric instances, they were worn singly, not in pairs.[83]

The mail shirt – Charlemagne's armour, as it was to be William of Normandy's – continued to have a long story. Adopted by the Arabs, by the mid thirteenth century through the Egyptian Mamluk dynasty the faith and ferocity of Islam reached the Sudan and Nigeria. Here, in the conserving ethos of African societies, the Sudanese continued to make and wear mail shirts up to this century. At the battle of Omdurman in 1898 the native cavalry wore mail as did their leader the Mahdi (with an iron helmet made in Birmingham), and in the 1950s a traditional Sudanese armourer made for an English anthropologist a shirt of iron mail that would have passed without comment on the battlefield of Hastings.[84]

Interlude – the horse as a princely gift

After this excursus on high-ranking horsemanship and its effects on the clothing appropriate for its performance in war and peace, we may return to the theme of the demonstration of power and prestige of the horse in harness for riding and, in a subsequent chapter, as draught for pleasure carriages. In the early Middle Ages of the west the Roman achievements in horse-breeding were taken up and stud farms early established with royal intent to maintain and improve a high standard of horse primarily for war, but also for personal display and ostentation as well as the aristocratic pastime of hunting. Early in this chapter I hinted that the horse from its close association with noble persons became on the one hand itself endowed with noble qualities, and on the other acquired as a member of the household the status of a pet. From pet to present was no great step and in the ancient as in the modern world the slippery slope in politics and commerce from diplomatic courtesy, ceremonial gift, douceur and consideration, bribe, squeeze and tip remained conveniently undefined in elusive morals and ethics. But as a high-level counter in the princely game of gift exchange, a large, well-bred and valuable horse had little to beat it in the post-classical world of competing states and principalities, all dependent on the majesty of fine horsemanship.

We have already seen how Roman horse-breeders turned not only east, beyond Thessaly to Persia amd Armenia, but also to North Africa and Spain, where improved chariot horses may have been introduced as early as the eighth century BC as well as riding horses by the Arab conquests of AD 641 onwards. Davis has pointed out the high regard with which Spanish horses were held as early as the 760s, and in 795 we saw Charlemagne's son Louis acquiring not only a shirt of mail but a fine horse in Spain. Notker the biographer of Charlemagne recorded, probably about 807, an embassy to the emperor from 'Persia', at that time a fief of the caliphate of Baghdad, in return for which 'the indefatigable Emperor sent a gift of Spanish

horses and mules to the ruler of the Persians'.[85] Such gift horses
would be the finest war horses then available, what would be known
as *dextrarius*, a destrier; the Great Horse, *magnus equus*. By the
twelfth century controlled and selective breeding in royal and
aristocratic stud farms had produced a range of horse types appropriate to the varied needs of society and distinctively named. About
1170 William Fitzstephen, a cleric in the entourage of Thomas Becket,
whose life he wrote and whose murder he witnessed, also wrote a
Description of London in which he gives a lively account of the
Friday horse fair held outside the city walls at Smithfield.[86] William
was a man with an ear for good Latin and an eye for good horseflesh,
and clearly knew what he was about. At the fair, he wrote, you saw
some five kinds of horse for sale. Under work horses would be the
summarius or pack-horse, and at a higher social level the pacing or
ambling horse, the palfrey or *gradarius* for the sedate riding of the
substantial citizen or lady or cleric. Then there are 'well bred younger
colts' still half trained, and *equos qui armigeris magis coveniunt*,
horses better suited to gentlemen, and finally *Hinc dextrarios
pretiosos elegantis formae*, here are the valuable destriers, fine limbed,
of good stature, ears twitching, necks arched and heavy rumped.
William was pleased with this passage, and gives an enlarged version
of it when describing in his Life of Becket a gift of three destriers
he himself made: it has echoes of Virgil.[87] We shall return to
Fitzstephen and Becket's state carriages in the next chapter; for the
present we leave him sizing up the horses at Smithfield and consider
the destrier for a moment more. Its qualities were those needed to
carry in appropriate aristocratic fashion an increasingly heavy load
of steel armour for both rider and mount. A mail shirt would weigh
only 11 kg (25 lb), whereas the full plate armour of the fifteenth and
sixteenth centuries was something like 22–27 kg (50–60 lb). The full
caparison and armour for man and horse at this time, with the
weapons of the knight, has been put at 196 kg (334 lb): the man's
riding weight must be added.[88] The packhorse load was 100–150 kg
(220–320 lb). The actual withers height of the war-horse probably
remained not much more than 150 cm (15 hands), but it had been
bred for other qualities, and obviously with success.

Such an animal, with its acquired characteristics of prestige and
nobility, was an obvious object of merit in ceremonial gift exchange.
Rare and exotic animals were much appreciated as royal presents in
medieval society. Elephants were esteemed exotics since Roman
times, and Charlemagne's elephant, presented to him by Haroun al

Rashid in 801, is famous. It started at Baghdad and came by ship to Porto Venere near Spezia, thence overland via Vercelli and over the Alps to Aachen, where it arrived in 802. Named Abu-l-Abbas it was made much of as a pet, and lived on for eight years. Other elephants were acquired, by the emperor Frederic II from the Holy Land in 1229, and St Louis gave one to Henry III of England (1216–1272) which was chronicled and drawn by Matthew Paris.[89] Lions, those most royal of beasts, were in great demand. The medieval master-builder and artist Villard de Honnecourt in France about 1235 was proud of having drawn a lion from life – *Et sacies bien qu'il fut contrefais al vif* he wrote on his heraldic and unlifelike drawing.[90] In England, the Lions in the Tower continued as a tourist attraction from the Middle Ages for centuries to come. Even stranger animals voyaged far as diplomatic gifts. In 1056 the first native bishop of Iceland came to Rome for his consecration by Victor II (by way of a reception by the emperor Henry III in 'Saxland'), bringing with him as an appropriately rare present, a polar bear from Greenland.[91] The custom of such presents of rare beasts between potentates is not extinct – one remembers Mr Richard Nixon and the Chinese pandas.

To return to the Great Horse as a princely gift, we may take two documented examples of European horses sent to oriental potentates, one in the mid fourteenth and the other in the early nineteenth century AD. After the conquests of Genghis Khan and Kublai Khan, by the mid thirteenth century a Mongol hegemony had been established in Asia from the Pontic to Peking, and travel by merchants and western Christian missionaries along regular routes was both safe and actively encouraged by the series of khanates ruling this huge area. As we shall shortly see, more than one Franciscan mission between 1240 and 1250 entered Central Asia and reported on its peoples. The journey was arduous and long. Writing about 1340 his handbook for merchants, Pegolotti reckoned that starting from the Crimea, it took 25 days by ox-wagon or 12 by horse-carriage to reach Astrakhan, another 45 days with pack-donkeys to the Ili river and another 70 days to the borders of China at Kansu, and thence a final 80 days to the capital Peking – a total of some 7 months.[92] It was a long way for a horse to walk.

Under circumstances which are not entirely clear, it appears that Usbeg Khan, at that time ruler of China (and one of the last Mongol emperors before the establishment of the Ming Dynasty in 1368) was in correspondence about 1338 with Pope Benedict XII. Usbeg had adopted the faith of Islam, but was tolerant of Christianity as well as concerned with western trade, and had made commercial treaties with Venice and Genoa about the same time. In his letter to the Pope he asked for his blessing and 'horses and other rarities of the sun-setting', as a result of which the Franciscan papal legate John of Marignolli was sent with gifts including 'a great war-horse' from Avignon to Cambalec (Peking) and arrived some years later, presumably having gone from Avignon by sea and thence to some Black Sea port and on more or less via Pegolotti's route. Christopher Dawson gives unsubstantiated additions to the episode, of the great size of the horse and the writing of an 'Ode to the Heavenly Horse' on its reception, and such an epithet would be, as we saw in the last chapter, appropriate to any fine horse from Ferghana westwards.[93] In 1415 the Chinese themselves, with an embassy to East Africa, sent a giraffe, a Heavenly Stag and a Heavenly Horse, anticipating the famous Admiral Zheng-He's expeditions of 1417–1433.[94]

From this presentation of a Great Horse by a Pope to a Mongol emperor, we may end with an incident of five hundred years later, the diplomatic gift by an English king to an Indian potentate of great horses in 1831. If much had changed between the Middle Ages and the reign of William IV, in one respect technology had remained static. Travel and transport on land was still dependent on the horse for riding or driving; agriculture remained wholly horse-powered. Much had gone into breeding varieties of stock that improved and amplified the range available to Fitzstephen at Smithfield Fair in 1170, and the destrier had been replaced as the aristocratic pleasure horse by the eighteenth century with breeding from the famous stallions of the early part of the century, the Godolphin Barb, the Darley Arabian and the Bierley Turk. The Thoroughbred was recognized as such by the *General Stud Book* of 1791. Carriages and wagons were improved to run on better road surfaces, with breeds of horse to match, and for the heavy commercial drays the Heavy Horse of today – Shire, Suffolk Punch and Clydesdale – had, by the end of the eighteenth century, been established by the efforts of improving breeders, such as Bakewell of Dishley, from what remained of heavy military stock ultimately of destrier origins.[95] It was 'five dappled grey dray horses' which were selected to be sent as a present to the Sikh Maharajah Ranjit Singh (who incidentally owned the Koh-i-Noor diamond), ruling the Punjab from Lahore, in 1831.

It was an unusual but inspired diplomatic gift. Historically India has had a curious position in horse breeding. After the chariot horses of the Vedic invasion in late prehistory had come in from the northwest, despite the contacts with such areas maintained by, for instance, the Kushans, for climatic or other reasons north India remained outside the world of active horse breeding. 'It is strange', writes the Indian historian Romila Thapar, 'that India never bred sufficient horses of quality, the best blood having always to be imported.' In the sixth century AD under the Guptas, fine horses were imported from Arabia, Iran and Bactria; by the thirteenth century the south Indian Chola kingdom was financing 'a vast trade in horses' from the Arab merchants 'of Hormuz and Kais, of Dhofar and Shihr and Aden'. Marco Polo writing about 1270–1290 noted this with surprise.[96] With such a background Ranjit Singh's taste was nicely calculated.

The 1831 mission was entrusted to a promising young political officer, Alexander Burnes, then aged twenty-five and well acquainted with India and its languages. He was later to be famous for his Central Asian travels, was knighted and was killed in Kabul in 1841.[97] A special ship took the five horses (and a carriage of which nothing more is heard) and on news of their arrival Ranjit Singh eagerly asked for one of the horseshoes to be sent to him 'accompanied by the most minute measurements of each of the animals'. On their arrival in Lahore he was not disappointed. He caused a complimentary letter to be written with his thanks to those who had arranged

to convey to me some horses of superior quality, of singular beauty, and elephantine stature . . . these animals, in beauty, stature and disposition, surpass the horses of every city and every country in the sun. On beholding their shoes, the new moon turned pale with envy, and nearly disappeared from the sky. Such horses the eye of the sun has never before beheld in his course through the universe.

Horses as gods and sacrifices

From Noble Animal to Divine Animal is an easy conceptual step, from admired qualities in the one to god-endowed or god-identification in the other. In what we know (or more often infer) of non-classical religion in late prehistoric and early historic pagan Europe horse deities take their place but are nowhere overwhelmingly or outstandingly important. As we saw earlier when considering riding side-saddle for women, a deity shared by both Roman and Gaulish religions was the goddess Epona. Her name is from the Gallo-Britonic *epo*-root, Greek *hippos* as against Latin *equus*, and she was the tutelary deity of mares and foals, donkeys and mules, the Lady of the Stables, benign on her side-saddle and with her links with fertility often implied by cakes, fruit or a cornucopia. Her name became a part of personal and place-names, but never in association with a warrior-god.[98]

One rider-god who seems to be Gallo-Roman but anonymous is the triumphant horseman trampling on a monster, a serpent-tailed giant, set on a column invariably dedicated simply to Jupiter Optimus Maximus and thickly distributed in an area of northeast Gaul, upper Germany and the Rhineland, all ancient Celtic territory. The figure does not seem merely a version of the Aurelian barbarian subduer, but rather a Celtic super-god who might be equated with some named deity like Taranis in one of his aspects.[99] Otherwise there is no evidence for horse deities playing any greater part in the Celtic pantheon than those equated with boars, stags, bears or other animals. The fine bronze horse from the Neuvy-en-Sulias Gallo-Roman sanctuary already referred to has a dedication to *Augustus Rudiobus*, an otherwise unknown deity, and is a stallion; the same sanctuary produced large figures of a boar and a stag.[100]

In commemorative sculpture the Roman Imperial cavalryman has a place in the hazily defined world between propaganda, the hero and the deity. The situation is epitomized in a well-known piece, the great 'distance slab' commemorating the beginning of the building of the Antonine Wall from Bridgeness in Scotland, of AD 142. Here the monumental inscription is flanked by two reliefs, one representing a legionary cavalryman triumphantly riding over a field *pl. 10* of native corpses and wounded, and on the other a portrayal of the sacrificial act of the *suovotaurilia*, the offering of a pig, a sheep and a bull-calf in a ceremony of purification associated with Mars. The theme of sanctified subjugation is implicit: in a later imperial conflict the symbols might have been a Bible and a Maxim gun. Moving from the general to the particular, a stock theme for the tombstones of cavalrymen is the horseman riding over a barbarian, not elegantly and symbolically like Marcus Aurelius, but energetically and brutally as in real life. Many of the surviving memorials are to Thracian auxiliaries, as Jocelyn Toynbee pointed out, and in Thrace, as we saw, the motif of the armed warrior on horseback goes back to the fourth century BC, and heroized or deified as the 'Thracian Rider' is a persistent theme in Romano-Thracian sculpture, to be adopted by the Eastern Church as the depiction of the heroic St George.[101]

In pagan Norse mythology horses are associated with Odin and the god Freyr and his consort-goddess Freyja as objects of sacrifice,[102] and it is now to the sacrifice and ritual of the slaughtered animals from Central Asia to northwest Europe, from prehistory to the Middle Ages, that we must now turn.

The sacrificial horse

The evidence for the sacrifice of horses in antiquity is both archaeological and literary, and the practice is either associated with burials or with ritual feasts in which horses were the animals eaten. The two may often merge – no burial is unaccompanied by some ritual – but horse-eating ceremonies with no funeral context can be inferred from archaeological evidence in prehistory from Europe and Asia, and are described by observers on the Siberian steppe until the beginning of the present century.

In all the sacrifices, funerary or simply ceremonial, the underlying concept is that of conspicuous waste and an admired display of wealth which, on the one hand, propitiate a god by the destruction of valuable objects (such as horses) and, on the other, aggrandize the owner, alive or dead, his family or office at a funeral by the destruction of valuables or sterilizing their function as status symbols by removing them from circulation in reciprocal gift display and exchange: from treasury to tomb. Here we have an emotional demonstration akin to the *potlatch* during life and forming a part of the general phenomenon of 'Royal Tombs'.[103] Broadly speaking the contexts of horse sacrifice are three. The first is where the horses are included among the deceased's valuables along with representatives of other domestic flocks and herds, or where a single riding horse is killed to accompany its owner. The number of animals varies, and when we come to the second group rises literally to hecatombs, where mass immolation has taken place on a prodigal scale. The third group is indicated archaeologically by hide burials, with the skin, skull, lower limb-bones and tail surviving when the carcass has been skinned to be cooked as a sacral meal, either as a part of a funeral ritual, or in a separate ceremony. What is of interest is that all three types of horse sacrifice are not only well documented archaeologically, but have been described by outside observers from Herodotus in the fifth century BC, to Christian and Arab writers in the Middle Ages from the tenth century AD to the mid fourteenth century. And hide sacrifices survived to be photographed by anthropologists.[94]

11 The Thracian Rider as St George. Textile printing block, probably last century, from Isfahan, Iran.

Horse burials in prehistory

We saw in Chapter I how paired ox-burials indicative of draught were being made in Neolithic Europe as early as the fourth millennium BC and in the Near East not much later, and in Chapter II how these became equids in the latter area when the horse came to replace the ox as a prestige draught animal. In the Sintashta River cemetery in the southern Urals of the mid second millennium BC, horses as well as horse-hide burials were associated with chariot graves, and in Shang China by 1200 BC charioteers with their horse team and chariot were being offered as funeral sacrifices. In the Celtic world of northwest Europe of the last four centuries or so BC, chariot burials in Gaul and Britain only quite exceptionally included the draught horses, though the paired horse burials of the pre-Roman Iron Age from British sites such as the Blewburton Hill hillfort in the Thames Valley imply chariot draught. Hide burials appear in the late pre-Roman Iron Age site of La Tène.[105]

When we turn to the horse as a prestige steed, the situation in the Scythian world of the fifth century BC on the Central Asian steppe shows a rather different pattern, illustrated by the Pazyryk burials in the Altai. Here we are in a horse-centred nomadic or semi-nomadic world which was in its essentials to survive until yesterday, where horses indicated status in herds rather than as individuals. Five of the princely Pazyryk graves contained horses sacrificed by pole-axing; ten in Barrow 1, seven in no. 2, fourteen in no. 4 and nine in no. 5. All were richly harnessed and caparisoned riding horses, except the four horses in Barrow 5 which were the team drawing the great prestige pleasure carriage found in the same tomb.[106] A greater profusion of sacrificed horses is found in the extraordinary tomb of Arzhan on the steppe in the Sayan Mountains of the Tuva autonomous republic 500 km west of Pazyryk, dating from about 250 years earlier in the seventh or eighth century BC.[107] Here a huge circular cairn, 110 m in diameter, drum-shaped and built over an elaborate radially compartmented timber construction, contained a central burial chamber, robbed but still containing the remains of a richly dressed man and woman, around which were six wooden dug-out coffins with burials of elderly men, each accompanied by his harnessed saddle-horse. Beyond these again were seven chambers containing a total of no less than 138 further horses, all old stallions, saddled and bridled. Finally on the periphery was a semicircle of over 300 small stone graves each containing a hide burial, evidently

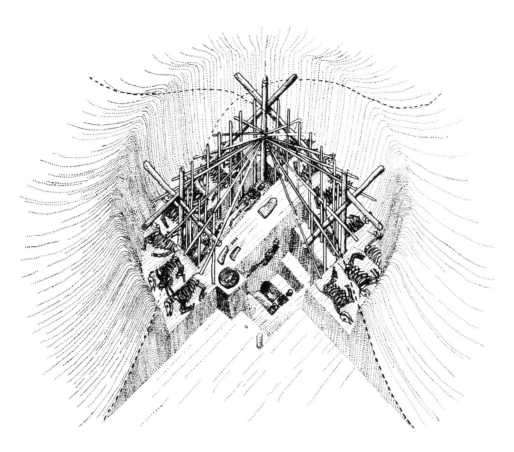

12 Scythian barrow with horse sacrifices, Kostromskaya, south Russia.

the remains of a huge ceremonial feast. In the central burial chamber, furthermore, the corpses lay on a floor strewn with horse tails and the hair of their manes. In all, something like not less than 450 or so horses had been sacrificed in a single princely funeral ceremony. This vast number is astonishingly excelled by a Chinese burial further still to the east, where at Zibo in central Shandong province a tomb of the Qi, a powerful vassal state of the Eastern Zhou dynasty in the fifth century BC was recently excavated. In a 5-m wide trench-grave on three sides of the tomb some 600 horses (they would have been chariot pairs) had been sacrificed and buried.[108]

These excessive figures are reduced in the classic Scythian tombs of the fifth and fourth centuries BC, though there were at least 360 sacrificed horses at Aul Ul' near Maikop, 35 at Tolstoya Mogila near Ordzhonikidze and 22 in the well-known Kostromskaya tomb.[109] This direct archaeological evidence confirms one of the most famous and remarkable accounts of elaborate funeral rites in antiquity, that of Herodotus of the Scythians. Well known though it is, it demands transcription here. At an early stage of his *History* he remarked in passing that among the Massagetae, east of the Caspian, 'the only god they worship is the sun, and to him they offer the horse in sacrifice' (I, 216), but later on Herodotus comes to his ethnographic description of the Scythians of the Crimea. 'On the river Dnieper,' he writes, 'when the king dies they dig a grave which is square in shape and of great size.' When it is ready they embalm the body and take it on a wagon through all the subject tribes

and so they come to the tombs of the kings. There the body of the dead king is laid in the grave prepared for it... and beams stretched above it to form a roof... In the open space around the body of the king they bury one of his concubines, first killing her by strangling, and also his cup-bearer, his cook, his groom, his lackey, his messenger, some of his horses, firstlings of all his other possessions and some golden cups... After this they set to work, and raise a vast mound above the grave, all of them vying with each other to make it as tall as possible (IV, 71).

When a year is gone by further ceremonies take place. Fifty of the best of the late king's attendants are taken... and strangled and fifty of the most beautiful horses. When they are dead, their bowels are taken out, and the cavity cleaned, filled full of chaff, and straightway sewn up again. This done, a number of posts are driven into the ground, in sets of two pairs each, and on every pair half the felloe of a wheel is placed archways; then strong stakes are run lengthways through the bodies of the horses from tail to neck, and they are mounted up upon the felloes... the legs dangling in mid air, each horse furnished with a bit and a bridle...the fifty strangled youths are then mounted severally on the fifty horses. To effect this a second stake is passed through their bodies along the course of the spine to the neck; the lower end of which projects from the body, and is fixed into a socket made in the stake that runs lengthwise down the horse. The fifty riders are thus ranged in a circle round the tomb, and so left (IV, 72).

Early medieval Europe

When we turn to pagan horse cults in early medieval Europe we must consider for a moment the unevenness of the adoption of Christianity from the fifth to the twelfth century. In Italy and southwest Gaul the Roman church survived the decay of the Empire and in the Celtic areas of the Atlantic façade the faith was adopted or, as in west Britain, survived from Roman times into the fifth century: Ireland was traditionally converted by St Patrick around 450. The pagan Frankish king Clovis was converted some time after 493 and the Anglo-Saxons in England Christianized from the 630s. In the north the Germanic peoples continued heathen until 960 in Denmark, about 1000 in Norway and Iceland, and well into the twelfth century in Sweden. In east Europe the situation was more complex. The Slavs were brought into the Church by about 800 as a result of Charlemagne's conquests of 796, when he also attacked and conquered the Avars, a semi-nomadic steppe people who had invaded and colonized the Hungarian plain within the Carpathian Ring in the 560s. They in their turn had been followed, again from the eastern steppes, by the Magyars in 893, defeated and Christianized by the Germans in 955.

For nearly half a millennium then the western Christians were flanked on their north and east by ancient heathen cults and belief-systems – Celtic, Nordic, Slav and from the mid sixth century those of the Asiatic steppe. It must be remembered too that the dates conventionally assigned to Christian conversion were usually no more than the adoption of the faith by a ruler and his court, while among the country people, the *pagani*, things went on much as before, as the early penitentials, such as that of Burchard Bishop of Worms of 1008–12, make clear. As a result, when Müller-Wille in 1970 made his masterly survey of horse-burials and offerings in early medieval Europe he was able to list over 560 instances between the fifth and the eleventh century from Iceland to the Danube, while excluding the Avar and Magyar sites to the east, of which nearly 300 were Merovingian and Ottonian.[110]

The horse burials of the Germanic north (including pagan Saxon England) were either horses or harnessing buried with the individual warrior-rider, or as separate horse-graves in human cemeteries. Others were burials under individual barrows, sometimes with adjacent post-structures such as four-post 'shrines'. In the rich tomb of Childeric I, the last great pagan Merovingian king who died in 481 and was buried at Tournai, was the severed head of his horse with its harness; recently, since Müller-Wille's corpus, new excavations near the site of the tomb by the church of St Brice disclosed three pits each containing ten complete horses, within 20 m of the royal tomb, and of its date.[111] These mass burials are exceptional; the burial of riding horses as personal property are a more obvious example of the conspicuous destruction of wealth as personal property as well as providing a status symbol for the afterworld. A good instance of such horse burials in a totally alien fourth-century context is to be found in Africa, in the royal tombs of the Blemyes of lower Nubia, a pagan people between Christian Abyssinia (from c.350) and Egypt (after about 390). Here, in the huge barrow cemeteries of Ballana and Qustul, the lavishly furnished princely tombs also contained burials of household possessions on a large scale – wives and concubines, slaves and dogs, oxen, camels, donkeys and richly caparisoned saddle horses with bridles and harness decorated in silver.[112]

In a discussion of horses from Avar and Magyar graves, Bökönyi points out that in common with the Germanic burials the animals were either stallions or geldings, and that whole animals were buried with the Avars, with only occasional hide burials, whereas in Magyar graves hide burials were the normal rite. (It will be recalled incidentally that the Avar burials contain the first stirrups in Europe.) Müller-Wille lists a number of hide burials from the Baltic, where connections with southeast Europe had been strong since Neolithic times.[113] Such burials as we saw at Arzhan in the eighth century BC presuppose a ceremonial feast with the communal eating of horse-meat, against which there has been a taboo in Europe at least since medieval times when, as an indication of the barbarity of the 'wild Irish', was quoted their eating of horseflesh. Such irrational prohibitions on certain arbitrary forms of meats and their preparation are common among many religions – for instance Jewish, Moslem and Hindu – where they are endowed with religious sanctions. In the case of the horse its secular avoidance, while partly a Christian reaction against pagan northern and eastern cults, may largely be due to its emotional and sentimental status as a high-class household pet.[114]

The ritual eating of a sacrificed horse, presupposed in archaeological form by hide burials, is historically attested in a well-known record from medieval Ireland. Writing in 1185 Giraldus Cambrensis in his *Description of Ireland* gives an extraordinary account of the traditional ritual performed to ratify the election of the 'king' of Conaile province in Ulster, an enthronement according to 'barbarous and abominable' ceremonies. At an assembly of the people a white mare was brought into their midst, whereupon the king ritually coupled with the horse, which was then killed, cut up and boiled. The king then got into the cauldron, and squatting in the horse-broth drank some, and ate some of the stewed meat. All this was done, concludes Giraldus in a neat phrase, *rite non recte*, according to custom rather than good morals. This ceremony has often been compared by Indo-European scholars to the Vedic *asvamedha* rite of royal consecration in ancient India, where at the climax of a year-long ceremony a sacred stallion is symbolically mated with the king's first wife and then sacrificed. But the no less significant feature of the horse-eating has not been stressed, and though the *hieros gamos*, the ritual marriage of horse-god to human, may be specifically Indo-European, the sacrificial horse-feast may have quite other and even more ancient roots.[115]

Horse and shaman

When Bökönyi and the Russian zoologist Zalkin were examining the horse remains from Scythian, Avar and Magyar graves they noticed a number of defective skeletons, lame or with abnormal incisor dentition visible in life. The obvious explanation was the saving of good stock by selecting poor or useless animals for sacrificial burial, but Bökönyi put forward a case for thinking that these abnormal horses were in fact to be regarded as endowed with the magic properties proper to those of shamans, as suggested by surviving Hungarian folklore. The ecstatic votaries within the belief-system of shamanism, widespread until recent times on the Asiatic steppe, had such horses attributed to them: 'it is not impossible', Bökönyi wrote, 'that these horses were the shamans' horses, animals to which extraordinary, magic powers were attributed, and that after the deaths of their masters they were put into the grave together'.[116]

Soon after this was published a very extraordinary burial of a man and a horse-hide in a tomb of Magyar date (early tenth century) was reported from Izsàk-Balázspuszta in Hungary. The man was evidently of high status, with a richly decorated saddle with silver fittings and trappings of belt, pouch, bow and quiver. The skull of the man, aged about twenty, was hydrocephalic (implying mental abnormality), with cleft palate, had deficient incisors and would have been hare-lipped; that of the horse was deformed so that in life it would have had an asymmetrical face, lolling tongue and foaming nostrils. It was about seven years old and only thirteen hands high. The archaeologists and osteologists agreed that rider and steed must have been 'frightening looking'. Together they were interpreted as a shaman and his magic horse.[117]

'Shaman' and 'shamanism' have often been used in a sense so vague as to be meaningless and applied to any manifestation of allegedly primitive elements in any religion. Since Mircea Eliade's exhaustive study there is little excuse for such misinterpretation. 'Shamanism', he wrote, 'in the strict sense is pre-eminently a religious phenomenon of Siberia and Central Asia . . . through the immense area comprising Central and North Asia, the magico-religious life of society centers on the shaman . . . he alone is the great master of ecstasy.' Originally documented in Asia it has also been recognized in North America and in all contexts among nomadic or semi-nomadic herdsmen and hunters rather than in agricultural sedentary economies, and in Central Asia among horsemen, where elaborate ceremonies took place comprising horse sacrifice and the shaman in trance ascending to the heavens on a visionary horse. These sacrifices, deliberately bloodless, take the form of offerings of horse hides with head and lower limb bones retained, to the supreme celestial Sky Gods: as Czaplicka put it, 'the bones and skin form the actual sacrifice. The flesh is consumed by those present at the ceremony'.[118] While features in common with such sacrifices can be recognized in Indo-European religions such as Celtic and Germanic, they are here by coincidence or more likely as traces of substrate beliefs. By its nature direct evidence is hard to pin-point, but the hunter-herdsman context of shamanism, and its distribution embracing Asia and North America, does suggest that we are faced with a situation which might be one of the final Palaeolithic, and the initial peopling of the New World from the Old.

It is with a background of longstanding shamanism that we should approach the records of Central Asian burial ceremonies with attendant horse sacrifices in the Middle Ages which so arrestingly survive in the accounts of Arab and Christian travellers from the west from the tenth to the fourteenth centuries AD, looking back to Herodotus and forward to the anthropologists' accounts of the last century.

Horses for Paradise

Contacts between western Christendom and the Mongol and Turkic peoples of the south Asiatic steppe were comparatively frequent from late Roman times. The opening up of regular trade and caravan routes was largely due to the activities of merchants from the west, and the famous Silk Route from Antioch to Luoyang was established in the third century AD. North of this seems to have run another route of earlier foundation in Scythian times which can be reconstructed from Herodotus, Aristeas of Proconnesus and Ptolemy, from the mouth of the Don by the southern Urals and the Altai Mountains, and thence to the mouth of the Yellow River.[119] This seems to have been the route taken by the Franciscan missionaries John of Piano Carpini and William of Rubruck between 1245 and 1255, to whose narratives we shall shortly come, and that sketched by Pegolotti. Along either route travellers would pass through territories politically Mongol or Turkic, with occasional Buddhist, Moslem or Nestorian Christian communities, but all deeply imbued with the ancient substrate beliefs and practices of shamanism.

In 921, at about the time the hideous young shaman and his misformed steed were mopping and mowing on the Hungarian *puszta*, the Abassid Caliph Al Muqtadir sent an embassy to the 'King of the Slavs' among the Oghuz Turks of the lower Volga which was reported on by the writer Ibn Fadlan, who gives a remarkably detailed eye-witness account of the burial of a chieftain of the 'Rus', usually taken to be Scandinavian merchants, though the ceremony is wholly that of the steppe. After a long account of the burial of the man with attendant sacrifices in a pit under a 'kind of clay dome', his people, continues Ibn Fadlan, 'betaking themselves to his horses, kill a hundred, two hundred or one of them according to their quantitites. They eat the flesh of these except the head, hoofs, hide and tail, which they suspend on wood. And they say "These are the horses on which he shall ride to Paradise."'[120]

The pagan Turkic Oghuz were absorbed by the middle of the eleventh century by another group of Turks from the east, the

Kipchaks, who were known to the Byzantines as *Komanoi*. These, the Comans or Cumans, remained in command of the Russian steppe until conquered by Genghis Khan in 1222 and became the Mongol Khanate of Kipchak (1237–1391). As the first Mongol people to be encountered by the traveller from the Christian west, 'Coman' was used loosely for all Mongol territory as far as the borders of China by mid-thirteenth-century travellers who described the funerary horse sacrifices in the shamanistic tradition in such detail.[121] These comprise two Franciscan missionaries, John of Piano Carpini and William of Rubruck, and a member of an embassy, Philippe de Toucy between 1245 and 1251, and later, from about 1330–1340, the North African Arab traveller, Ibn Battuta.

Carpini started on his mission from Pope Innocent IV to the Mongol Guyuk Khan from Lyons in 1245: his objective was the Mongol capital at Karakorum, on the river Orkhon west of Ulan Bator.[122] Travelling through Poland and Galicia he left Kiev for Coman territory by February 1246, and, along the 'Scythian Route' north of the Caspian and the Aral Seas, by Lake Ala Kul in Dzungaria and so to the Khan's camp, the Syra Orda, half a day's journey from Karakorum. He prefaced his *History of the Mongols* with a general description of the country and its peoples, and in Chapter III gives an account of their burial rites. The chief men are buried secretly in a hidden royal precinct 'so that no one may discover the spot afterwards', but

if he is one of the less important men he is buried in secret in the open country wherever it seems good to them. He is buried with one of his dwellings, sitting in the middle of it, and they place a table in front of him, and a dish filled with meat and a goblet of mare's milk. And they bury with him a mare and her foal and a horse with bridle and saddle, and another horse they eat and fill its skin with straw, and this they stick up on two or four poles...The bones of the horse which they eat they burn for the men's souls...They also bury gold and silver in the same way with a dead man; the cart in which he rides is broken up and his dwelling destroyed.

William of Rubruck,[123] another Franciscan, was sent on a similar embassy in May 1253 by Louis IX of France (St Louis), then campaigning at Acre, to the court at Karakorum where on Guyuk's death Mongka had become Great Khan. Rubruck went by Constantinople to the Crimea and thence to the Lower Volga and eastwards on more or less Carpini's route. Like him, he prefaced the account of his journey by a general account of the 'Tartars', and when he comes to burial customs also distinguishes the secret precinct of the nobility from that of others, going on:

The Comans make a great mound over the dead man and set up a statue to him, facing the east and holding a cup in his hand in front of his navel...I saw a man recently dead for whom they had hung up, between tall poles, the skins of sixteen horses, four facing each quarter of the earth, and they had put cosmos [*koumis*] for him to drink and meat for him to eat.

Something of the Comans was already known at Acre by 1251, when Philippe de Toucy had gone on an embassy to them from Constantinople. He 'told us of a most amazing spectacle he had witnessed while in the Coman camp,' wrote Joinville.

A knight of very high rank among them having died, they had dug a grave, very deep and wide in the earth. In it they had placed the knight, very richly attired and seated in a chair; they had also lowered the best horse he had, and his first sergeant, in to the grave alive. Then the mouth of the grave was covered by throwing closely fitting boards across it. Meanwhile all the men in the army had run to get stones and earth, and before going to sleep that night they had raised a great mound above the tomb.[124]

Other medieval writers on the Central Asian Mongols such as the Jew Benjamin of Tudela (1160–1163), the Franciscan Odoric (1318–1330) or Marco Polo, make no mention of horse burials or sacrifices, but writing about 1342 the Arab traveller Ibn Battuta described the burial of a Mongol khan in some detail.[125] Ibn Battuta was a Moslem from Tangier, a member of 'the religious upper class' who at the age of twenty-one embarked on the statutory Islamic pilgrimage to Mecca in 1325 and, becoming infatuated with travel in strange parts, ended up visiting China, India, Malabar and West Africa. He returned to Fez in 1349 and sixteen years later wrote an account of his experiences. While always entertaining he is not always to be relied on for his accuracy, and Gibbs, his editor, shows that the circumstantial account of what he claimed to be an eye-witness account of the Mongol emperor of China's burial at Peking in about 1342 cannot have happened: the emperor Togon Timur reigned from 1333 to 1371. What he describes must have been either a generalized account or more likely the burial of another Mongol khan. What he reported runs as follows:

A great *na'us*, that is a subterranean chamber, was dug for him and richly furnished. The khan was laid in it with his weapons and all the gold and silver plate from his palace was deposited in it with him. With him also were put four slave girls and six of the principal mamluks, who carried drinking vessels, then the door of the chamber was built up and the whole thing covered with earth until it reached the size of a large mound. After that they brought four horses and drove them on to the khan's grave until they stopped, then they set up a wooden erection over the grave and suspended the horses from it, having first driven a piece of wood through each horse from tail to mouth. The above-mentioned relatives of the khan were also placed in subterranean chambers along with their weapons and house utensils, and they impaled over the tombs of the principal members, of whom there were ten, three horses each, and over the tombs of the rest, one horse each.

Taken together these remarkable narratives from the tenth to the fourteenth century AD give a consistent picture of the shamanistic horse sacrifices of Central Asia, which so vividly embody the archaeological inferences one would make from sites such as Arzhan in the eighth century BC and the account of Herodotus in the fifth. And so, when in the secular west Jordanus Ruffus was celebrating the nobility of the princely horse, on the Mongol steppes the shamans had raised it to the status of a sacred steed, to be sacrificed to the gods as a magic horse to carry kings to the other world.

IV
From Chivalry to Carriage

We have now seen how from the beginning of the western Middle Ages the ridden horse had become established as the vehicle of prestige and authority for all men from king to commoner each in his degree. At the lowest level of the social scale it presented itself as the only alternative to walking for any individual journey not necessitating the transport of anything more than personal belongings, and so it remained until the invention and adoption of the bicycle in the 1890s. For merchandise, official military and civil supplies, transport was provided on land by pack-horses or horse-drawn wagons, carts or exceptionally sledges on the farm or for long-distance road transport, and these could also be used on occasion for the sick, infirm, old or dead, and most important, they became appropriate for the conveyance of ladies and of the higher clergy. From these last functions the concept of travel for pleasure by vehicle arose, and the wheeled carriage dedicated not only to utilitarian ends but for comfort and enjoyment established itself, as the world moved into more civilized manners.

In barbaric societies male convention demanded overt statements of masculinity in conditions where warfare between nation states, political factions, religious sects, families or relatives, was an accepted part of everyday life, and physical force often a condition of success or survival. The warrior thus becomes the hero, athletic and tough, arrogant and proud, with kings and princes heading the social scale, the embodiment of the martial virtues no less than the skills of statecraft. Perhaps behind this cherished myth still lay unconscious the ancient identification of king and country in vital qualities, Frazer's theme of 'divine kings on whose life the fertility of men, of cattle, and of vegetation is believed to depend'.[1] However conceived, the myth could be uniquely maintained by the horseman, by virtue not only of his valorous self, but by the high status gained by his steed, which elevated him, socially as well as literally, above the commoners of an acutely stratified hierarchy ordained and maintained by God. To be conveyed on wheels, or worse still in comparative comfort under cover, was a manifest sign of weakness in a tough and competitive man's world emerging from barbarism and scornful of comforts it did not understand.

The military needs for cavalry and transport extended well beyond the Middle Ages and into the European wars of the sixteenth to eighteenth centuries. The early modern field is well covered, notably in Joan Thirsk's classic Stenton Lecture of 1977 and the late Ralph Davis's study of the medieval warhorse in 1989, and for our purposes only a few points may be stressed.[2] The reserve of military horses was maintained and improved through official action by the Crown and the encouragement of the nobility and gentry in setting up stud farms. Dr Thirsk makes the point I have already, in Chapter II, characterized by the Price of Prestige incident on any maintenance of horses, whether for chariot draught or for prestige riding. She is able to give figures where I could only infer expenditure of labour – 98 servants to look after 119 horses for Henry VIII; 83 men for 98 horses in Elizabeth I's stables; at a time when a labourer's wage was 3s 4d a week, fodder for a horse was assessed at 5s for 14 lbs of hay a day, 7 lbs of straw, a peck of oats and half a peck of peas. These are interesting figures to set against the ration figures of Kikkuli in the second millennium BC or Polybius in the second century BC.

Henry VIII's demands for horses to maintain his wars in France and Scotland were enormous, to be reckoned in tens of thousands on occasion, drawing not only on Britain but the allied Low Countries. He also bought or acquired by gift in the time-honoured manner fine horses from Spain and Italy, and from 1535 promoted three Acts of Parliament 'concernyng the breeds of Horses' and 'the great decay of the generation and bredyng of good swyfte and strong Horses'. This was to be done (as Davis put it) by 'an appeal to snobbery' which 'equated social status and wealth' in the ordinance that owners of enclosed parks with high incomes and wives who wore 'any gown of silk...bonnet of velvet, with any habiliment, paste or egg of gold, pearl or stone, or any chain of gold' should breed and provide horses of a required standard, ultimately for the Crown: the Price of Prestige indeed. The standards were, in perspective, modest enough: the first Act demanded mares of 'the hieght of xiii handfulles at the lest', the 1540–42 Acts raising this to

14 hands for mares and 15 for stallions, well within the domesticated horse range of prehistory and hardly exceeding the modern pony class.

For uses less demanding than war and fitting the domestic needs of nobility, gentry and the middling people, training in the ambling or pacing gait was a desirable characteristic to be induced and maintained as a part of horse-training from medieval times onwards, together with the walk, trot and gallop appropriate to war and the civil pursuits of more energetic riding, hunting with hounds or hawk and by the end of the sixteenth century, racing. Already by 1170 William Fitzstephen was eying appreciatively not only the destriers in the horse-fair, but riding horses *suaviter ambulantes pedibus, lateraliter simul erectus quasi a subalternis et demissis,*[3] four hundred years later Thomas Blundeville in 1565 commended 'a race of fine ambling horses to travaile by the way...the mare to be also a bastard Jennet bred here in this realm, having an ambling pace, or some other of our ambling mares.' Chaucer by the 1380s assigned appropriate mounts to his Canterbury pilgrims with as nice a sense of social ranking as the riders themselves, from knight and franklin to miller and seaman, parish priest, prioress and the redoubtable Wife of Bath, both of whom would have ridden side-saddle in the chair-set-sideways as we saw in the last chapter. Early achieved, the technology of the ridden horse remained of its nature virtually static, with or without stirrups and rigid saddle. The tradition of manuals of horsemanship[4] likewise continued over the centuries from Xenophon through Vegetius, Rabanus Maurus and Jordanus Ruffus (discussed in the last chapter) and into the Renaissance in Italy, where Federico Grisone's *Giordini di Cavalcare* on 1550 was regarded as the new Xenophon:

> If Xenophon deserude imortall fame,
> Or Grison's glorie from earth to sky did reach...

opens Sir John Tracy's commendatory verses to Christopher Clifford's *The Schoole of Horsemanship* (1585): Xenophon was printed in Italy in Greek in 1516, in Latin in 1539. Grisone was translated by Thomas Blundeville between 1559 and 1564, who published his own book, *The Foure Chiefest Offices belonging to Horsemanship* in 1565. The manuals continued to be published in France and England, with William Cavendish, Duke of Newcastle, renowned for his *General System of Horsemanship and all its Branches* of 1667.

But already by the seventeenth century comfortable travel appropriate to monarch and court, nobility and gentry, and the growing well-to-do middle class was being offered in a new and seductive form, the horse-drawn closed carriage. In the next sections I propose to return to prehistory and the European origins of the four-wheeled carriage, with a glance at the contrasted oriental tradition, and then trace subsequent developments in the western Middle Ages into the vehicle which the sixteenth and seventeenth centuries at first regarded as an unwelcome novelty, the coach. It was to be attacked by pamphleteers and vested interests like the watermen, and regarded by the conservative gentry with indignant contempt. John Aubrey around 1660 recorded the choleric outburst of Thomas Tyndale, an old gentleman of a type still with us – 'Alas! O' God's will! Now-a-dayes every one, forsooth! must have coaches, forsooth! In those days [temp. Elizabeth] gentlemen kept horses...This made the gentry robust and hardy and fitt for service...Our gentry forsooth in these dayes are so effeminated that they know not how to ride on horse-back.' Aubrey himself agreed. 'Now we are come all to our coaches, forsooth! Now young men are so farre from managing good horses, they know not how to ride a hunting nag...In Sir Philip Sydney's time 'twas as much a disgrace for a cavalier to be seen in London rideing in a coach in the street as now 'twould be to be seen in a petticoate and waistcoate.'

But riding could have its hazards for the pompous. It was to Aubrey in 1656 that Canon Watts of Hereford Cathedral told the story of Dr Price, the Dean, and it forms an appropriate tailpiece to the story of prestige horses.

This deane was a mighty pontificall proud man, and that at one time when they went in procession about the cathedrall church, he would not doe it the usually way in his surplice, hood, etc., on foot, but rode on a mare, thus habited, with the Common-Prayer booke in his hand, reading. A stone-horse happening to break loose, and smelt the mare and ran and leapt her, and held the Reverend Dean all the time so hard in his embrace, that he could not get off till the horse had done his businesse. But he would never ride in procession afterwards.[5]

From chariot to pleasure-car in the ancient East

Before turning to our main theme, the evolution of the closed carriage which was first to rival and before long to supplant the ridden horse in the west, we may briefly review the transformation of the war-chariot into the two-wheeled pleasure-car in the Orient, beginning with India. Here we are dependent on a few models and ambiguous sculpture implying canopied vehicles which could hardly be used in battle but suggest parade or pleasure. From the Indus Valley city-sites of Harappa and Chanhu-daro come two almost identical copper models of cars, drawn by a pair of probable equids rather than oxen, with a driver sitting forward of the box with open gabled awning for a passenger. The stratigraphy of these models is uncertain, but they probably belong to the secondary occupation on both sites, at the close of the second millennium BC. A few other later models of canopied chariots from for instance Brahmapuri, of the second century AD, have been published. The little canopied *ekka* still survives in rural India.[6]

For China the evidence is more abundant and better documented. Here, as we saw at the end of Chapter II, the chariot as early as the eighth century BC was being thought of as much an object of elegant ornament as a war-engine, and by at least the first century the chariot adorned by a fixed parasol was in use, hardly a vehicle for the rough and tumble of the battlefield. The parasol as royal status-symbol has an interesting history both in the Orient and in the west, as Jean Macintosh has shown.[7] Carried as an emblem of sovereignty it appears in Assyrian art and in a relief of Sennacherib (705–681 BC), it is being held over the king's head in a chariot – a scene of parade and ceremony, not of active warfare – and for the figures in procession of Darius and Xerxes in fifth-century Persepolis. In China the fixed parasol is found on model chariots from Majuzi in the first century BC and Leitai about AD 200, and thence representations carry it into Han and beyond, side-by-side with numerous open canopies. It was brought by Greek orientalizing to the west, where a two-wheeled open pleasure car is shown with a fixed parasol in an oddly Chinese manner in an Archaic Etruscan relief of the sixth century BC at Poggio Civitate (Murlo). As a final oriental postscript the royal parasol came to be shown borne above medieval popes from at least the twelfth century following Byzantine custom, traditionally segmented red and yellow (like a miniature golf umbrella).[8]

The Chinese representations show various forms of canopies and awnings. A fine Han Dynasty stone relief of the late second century AD shows an elegant parasol-canopied vehicle, two-wheeled and drawn by a single horse between shafts, with passenger and driver sitting side-by-side, and a simple inscription 'The Gentleman's Chariot'. That traditional figure of honour, the Confucian Gentle-

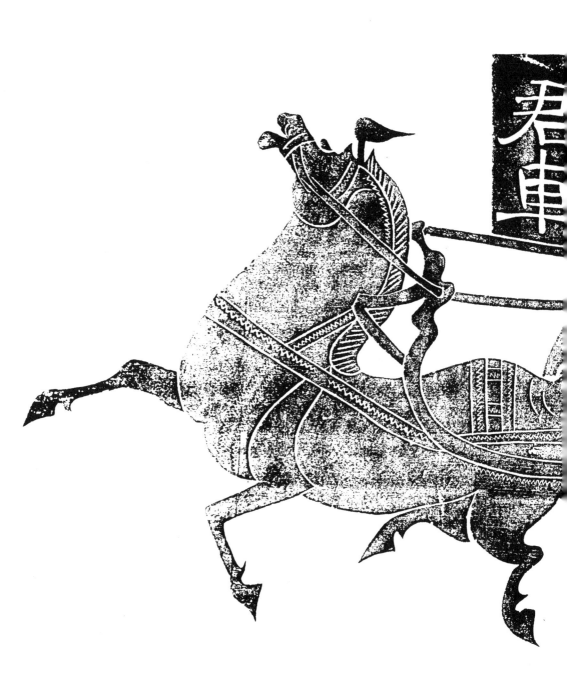

*13 Covered pleasure chariot with inscription 'The Gentleman's Chariot'.
Rubbing of Chinese Han Dynasty stone relief.*

man, scholarly and courteous, just and wise, is here accorded the appropriate pleasure-car of prestige in a civilized society. There are also Han illustrations of utilitarian tilt-covered carts of a type we shall see also played a part in the west. But a unique find is the astonishing half-size bronze model of a covered carriage from one of the effigy-pits in the precinct of the tomb of the first Qin emperor Shi Huang who died in 210 BC – the famous 'Tomb of the Terracotta Warriors'. This model shows in great detail what is in effect a miniature house with wide eaves on two wheels, drawn by four pottery horses. Roughly contemporary pottery models of houses are known, but the Shi Huang model is a unique representation of the earliest closed coach.[9] The early adoption of parasols, awnings and canopies on vehicles originating as war chariots show a different and more civilized attitude to comfortable travel than the warrior's ethos of tough masculinity of the west. As Mary Littauer put it in a different but allied context, the early Chinese 'had no long-held horseman's tradition; a high-arched saddle or a stirrup would not be for them a symbol of womanish weakness, the national reverence for age would preclude any prejudices due to its infirmities.'[10] The development of the two-wheeled covered or shaded pleasure-car in early China is not therefore surprising, reflecting the favourable atmosphere for ease and elegance among the aristocracy of the day.

The Pazyryk ceremonial carriage

To the northwest of the ancient state of China, 3000 km away, lie the Altai Mountains and Steppe, where at Jamani-Us, among a group of rock carvings of chariots, are a couple of canopied cars in the Han style.[11] In the Altai, too, lie the famous frozen barrow tombs of Pazyryk, of the fifth century BC, already referred to in Chapter II, *pl. 11* and in Barrow 5 was a surviving four-wheeled carriage, which we must now consider in greater detail.[12] Rudenko published a fairly full account but no measured drawings, so that some points are uncertain. It is 3.3 m in overall length, the wheel base (axle to axle) 1.65 m, the overall length of the axle-bed and arms 3.36 m. The four wheels are each 1.6 m in diameter, with elaborate long naves giving an approximate gauge of 2.2 m, and each pair linked by an exterior bar. They have single-piece bent felloes and 34 spokes, and like the rest of the carriage are of birch wood, with birch-bark bindings at the junction of spokes and nave. The body is of lightly framed rod-and-wickerwork construction. The driver's seat forward of a

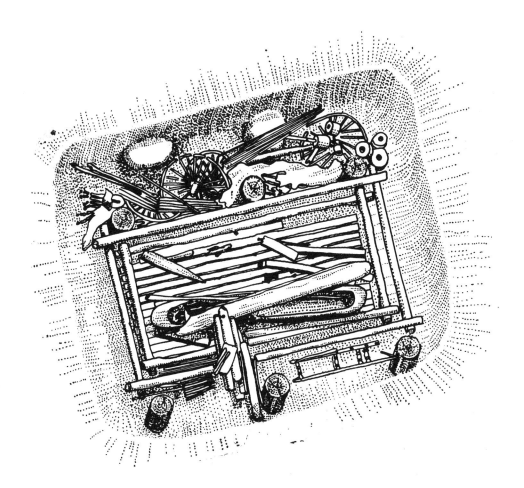

14 The carriage grave at Pazyryk, in the Altai.

canopied passenger compartment 1.3 by 2.0 m, with rod uprights 1.2 m or more high carrying a plank roof. It had black felt curtains and Rudenko thought it was crowned with the figures of four swans of coloured felt, white, black, yellow and red, stuffed with deer's hair and some 30 cm long. Traces of red paint survived on the bodywork. A draught-pole 3.2 m long was lashed forward of the front axle 'by means of a special bow' to allow for some flexibility for a team of four horses, two harnessed by a yoke and yoke-saddles and an outer pair by traces. It is one of the most remarkable vehicles surviving from antiquity, after conservation standing today intact in the Museum of the Hermitage in Leningrad.

As we saw in Chapter II, technologically the Pazyryk carriage looks to both west and east. As a four-wheeler it reflects the tradition of the Caucasian and South Russian solid-wheeled ox wagons of the third and second millennium BC, rather than the two-wheeled chariot and cart types universal in China from Shang times onwards. The huge wheels on the other hand have close parallels in those of the actual chariots of the Shi Huang effigy-pits (apparently totalling at least 70), with diameters of 1.8 m and some 34 spokes,[13] of 210 BC. The large number of spokes occur westwards at Lchashen in the Caucasus (28) where the wheel gauge is 1.7 m as against 2.2 m at Pazyryk, which however falls within the Chinese range in the Shang and Zhou dynasties. The use of birch-bark binding recalls Egypt in the second millennium BC. Finally the use of yoke-saddles in harnessing is in common on the one hand with the Chinese chariot-burials and in the west with Egyptian chariots and the Mycenaean Linear B pictographs. The decorative canopy seems wholly Chinese and quite distinct from the arch-tilted ox-wagons of the Caucasus and Mesopotamia. All in all, the Pazyryk carriage offers a remarkable link between eastern and western traditions of prestige transport. Rudenko stressed the strictly ceremonial function of the carriage in a terrain unsuited to wheeled traffic of any kind, let alone a vehicle with two rigidly fixed axles and incapable of the least flexibility in turning.

Wagon and carriage in the west

We can now leave China and the Near East and turn to Europe, where a wholly independent tradition of vehicle building and use established itself from at least the sixth century BC and can thenceforward be followed continuously up to the advent of the motor car, as the main centres of technological innovation shifted irrevocably from the ancient East to ancient Europe. The eastern convention of pleasure-carriages derived from the two-wheeled chariot for war and parade, but in the west an independent sequence based on a sophisticated horse-drawn carriage or wagon with four spoked wheels looked back ultimately to the ox-drawn vehicle with four disc wheels, which as we saw in Chapter I represented the earliest wheeled transport in Europe, going back to the fourth millennium BC.

The chariot tradition continued in barbarian Europe, from Gaul and Britain to Thrace, up to the Roman conquests, and in the classical world itself for the increasingly specialized functions of ceremonial parade, and racing. But by the eighth century BC in Greece, four-wheeled carriages, with spoked wheels, shallow open body and paired horse draught, are being depicted, together with chariots, by Geometric vase painters.[14] In central and western continental Europe from the seventh, and particularly the sixth, century BC a rich series of ceremonial carriages of similar type have survived in burials of the early Iron Age (technically Hallstatt D): over 240 are known, distributed from Burgundy to Bohemia, from the Alps to Alsace, and by the second century BC their counterparts are found in graves and votive deposits as far north as Denmark. Publication ranges from the early nineteenth century to today, and in striking contrast to the sad story of inadequate field techniques and publication we encountered with the South Russian ox-wagons, standards have been very high.[15] Side-by-side with the actual vehicles, the representations in rock engravings in the Alps and again in South Scandinavia, and on pottery, confirm in detail the constructional features of the originals.

Taken as a group the sixth-century BC Hallstatt carriages are of remarkably uniform type and even dimensions. The body undercarri- *pl. 12* age was long and relatively narrow, averaging 1.8 to 2.0 m long by 70 cm wide, and its construction that of two axle-trees joined by a central Y- or trident-shaped member (technically a 'perch') traceable in several surviving vehicles and explicit in many representations. The spoked wheels, 90 to 70 cm in diameter, had bent wood or segmental felloes (sometimes both combined) with iron hoop tyres and stud nails; spoke numbers varied but most were between 6 and 10. On the axles-and-perch undercarriage rested, apparently without permanent means of attachment, a shallow tray-like body, its sides, like the wheels and their massive moulded naves frequently

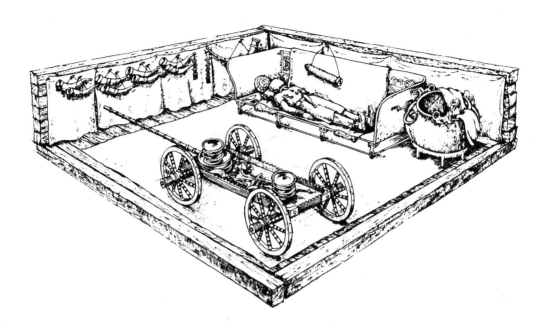

*15 Reconstructed grave with carriage, Hallstatt D, about 500 BC,
found at Hochdorf near Stuttgart.*

ornamented with elaborately decorated bronze or iron sheathing, as could also be the draught-pole.

This and the traction mechanism is of some importance as it is linked with a crucial point in the technological history of all four-wheeled wagons or carriages, their ability to turn with a pivoted front axle. Postponing discussion of this for a moment, the Hallstatt carriages, horse-drawn as the evidence of bits as well as the depictions show, continued to use, as in chariotry, paired draught harnessed by yoking to a pole. Now a two-wheeled cart or chariot can tilt with impunity, whereas a wagon or chariot must maintain the rear and fore pairs of wheels firmly horizontal on the travelling surface, and so provision for some vertical play of the draught-pole is essential. In the Hallstatt four-wheelers, a Y-shaped pole, with two arms fixed ahead of the front axle, allowed for such vertical movement, and gave with the whole perch and pole undercarriage structure a double Y plan view. This view, shown in the conventional vertical viewpoint by barbarian European art and featuring the structure of the undercarriage, may be related to the unattached tray-like body, which could be a temporary adjunct to be used or dispensed with according to circumstances. In the eighth-century BC carriages shown in profile in Greek Geometric art conventions, a similar shallow body is shown. An important point revealed by new study of the Hallstatt vehicles is that they had been functional carriages of standing before they reached the princely grave as a prestige symbol, and not newly made *ad hoc* hearses.

The pivoted front axle from prehistory to history

The essential technology for an effective four-wheeled vehicle in practical everyday use is provision for the front axle-and-wheels unit to turn laterally and independently of the rear wheels and body. We know from surviving vehicles and infer from models that fixed-axle ox wagons were in fact in use in ancient Mesopotamia, the Caucasus, South Russia and Central Europe from about 3000 to 1500 BC and survived until the fifth century BC at Pazyryk in Central Asia. Such a fixed-axle type cannot therefore be dismissed as a practical vehicle on the farm, for instance, or for limited occasions of parade and ceremony. Discussion of the use of the pivoted axle in the Middle Ages was initiated in a frequently quoted paper by Marjorie Boyer in 1960,[16] in which she wrote, 'Four-wheeled vehicles with the pivoted front axle came in at least by the time of the Hallstatt Iron Age in the second millennium BC and it is well established that the ancient Romans knew and employed this technological advance.' This unfortunate statement has stood to mislead historians for thirty years: Hallstatt is, of course, sixth century and not second millennium BC, and nothing is known of the technology of Roman vehicles save what can be inferred from the iconography of lateral views on reliefs, mosaics and coins. The first error is trivial and due to using archaeological sources obsolete in 1960 and still more so today. The second, as we saw in Chapter I, arises from the confident acceptance in secondary sources of the unwarranted 'reconstructions' derived from the coach-builder Ginzrot in 1812. Incidentally the Hallstatt examples known before 1960 include two reconstructions we can now see as misleading, that of Ohnenheim (1921) and of Bell (1948). Today we know more of the basic constructional details of the Hallstatt carriages than we do of either Roman or medieval vehicles in the lack of archaeological survival and consequent dependence on lateral artistic depictions.

When in 1983 I came to consider the question of the pivoted front axle in Hallstatt D carriages, I found all previous studies had assumed that to allow any turning of the front axle, the undercarriage must allow of the passage of the two front wheels wholly or partially beneath it, and that they should as a result often be smaller in diameter than the rear pair, which in the Hallstatt vehicles was never the case. This assumption ignored the critical factor, well known to students of nineteenth-century farm wagons, of the 'lock' obtainable with a pivoted front axle, particularly the quarter-lock 'in which the movement of the wheels is limited by the straight sides of the wagon floor'. With the Y-shaped perch held rigidly on the rear axle by the arms, a simple locking bolt at the fore end will enable the axle to pivot, and with the relatively narrow body and wide gauge, a respectable angle of turn of 20 degrees and a turning circle of about 8.5 m could be calculated for a specific Hallstatt four-wheeler.[17] With the recognition of the quarter-lock, the effective use of a pivoted front axle is simplified, and could have been transmitted in Europe from the sixth century BC to the sixth century AD and beyond into the Middle Ages, to be modified only by the use of the rigid horse-collar and shaft rather than pole-and-yoke harnessing, and the use of the whipple-tree. Summing up the evidence, iconographical and textual, in 1960 Dr Boyer could find no clear evidence for pivoted front axles until the second half of the fourteenth century in medieval Europe. This excludes the potentialities of the quarter-lock and leaves open the possibility of transmission from the pre-Roman Iron Age. Our complete ignorance of most of vehicle technology in classical times, as we saw, creates an insurmountable barrier. Technological development may be regressive as well as progressive, and earlier achievements forgotten or dismissed. In vehicle technology we must remember the deliberate abandonment of all wheeled transport by the Islamic world from the seventh century to the nineteenth, when in 1835 Kinglake could still contrast 'wheel-going Europe' with the Ottoman world of riders and pack animals. Much of late prehistoric technology was lost by medieval times – the fine wheelwright's craft of the bent felloe and shrunk-on hoop tyre, the latter replaced by segmental strakes and not to be re-invented until the end of the eighteenth century. The pivoted front axle, in an impoverished technology, could similarly have been forgotten, to be achieved afresh in full medieval times.

In our pursuit of the prestige pleasure-carriage in the west, we retain the thread of technological continuity in the working cart and wagon on the farm, as with the collapse of Roman civic culture an agrarian and ultimately manorial economy took the place of the towns. Here the immediate successors of the solid-wheeled and almost certainly fixed-axle *plaustrum* of the Roman world would continue to perform its limited duties in an economy where travel was restricted and roads few and bad. It can hardly be due to coincidence and re-invention that the farm wagon of pre-industrial modern Europe should, with its forked perch undercarriage structure, repeat Hallstatt prototypes. The draught pole with yoke harnessing continued with ox carts in the Atlantic west until today,[18] and with horses and collar and trace harnessing, a Y-shaped pole is shown in a German woodcut of 1483 on a tilt-covered carriage shown overturned.[19] The A-framed cart with paired draught, prehistoric and recent in the Caucasus, recent in Anatolia, Sardinia and Portugal, is attested in medieval England by drawings in an eleventh-century manuscript.[20] As we saw at the end of Chapter II, harnessing with shafts was invented in China by the fifth century AD coupled with the rigid horse collar, and in the west the earliest representation of the collar (with traces) is usually taken to be that in the Trier Apocalypse of *c*.800.[21] The Romans experimented with shafts, but probably their medieval adoption from the tenth, and more certainly the twelfth, century is an example of re-invention.[22] Thereafter they are virtually universal.

Two short French essays are frequently quoted in earlier vehicle studies; both are characterized by sweeping generalizations and scanty documentation, and review vehicle distribution with small-scale sketch maps. For pre-Industrial Europe (modified in a later map by Jenkins)[23] a broad dichotomy is seen between a huge Mid Continental Wagon Zone extending westwards effectively to the Rhine, Low Countries and southern England, flanked to the south and north by South and North European Cart Zones, coastal to the Mediterranean and the Atlantic façade. Broadly speaking this post-medieval distribution is dictated by geography and terrain, with the four-wheelers appropriate to the plains and the two-wheelers to the hilly and rocky coastal fringes. There is of course considerable marginal overlapping, especially in England, and in our pursuit of the origins of the medieval pleasure carriage, we must consider both forms of vehicles as prototypes. Our final background material is to be sought in both carts and wagons with a covered superstructure or tilt.

Tilt-wagons and carts in antiquity

The use of arched coverings to vehicles goes back as we saw to the very beginnings of wheeled transport in the Near East and the Caucasus, and is such an obvious device that we need not seek for any relationships when it appears for instance in Han and later China as well as the west. A good Han example is shown in a relief of AD 193 at Yi-nan, with all the detail of the tunnel-shaped covering of a cart, with fabric or leather neatly tied by cords over the hoops of the frame. Classical Greek used a word *harmamaxa* for a covered four-wheeler, regarded as of Persian origin and assigned by Xenophon to women's use. Strabo writing of the Gauls uses the word for transport wagons up the Rhône Valley, presumably covered, and again quite explicitly of the Cimbri of Jutland, where during battles the priestesses 'beat on the hides that were stretched over the wicker bodies of the wagons'.[24] In the Roman west we noted in Chapter I the vehicle known as the *carpentum* or 'two-wheeled covered carriage in which Roman matrons in early times, and later state priestesses had the privilege of driving through the city on a feast-day and the day preceding', and if we accept the plausible equation of the *carpentum* and the vehicle shown in commemorative coins such as the sestertii of Agrippina I and II, this is an elaborately decorated tilt-cart drawn by mules. Whatever it was called in Latin, the utilitarian version of the tilt-cart was in use in the provincial countryside as in the relief at Klagenfurt in Carinthia.[25] We shall shortly see the part played by the long tilt-wagon as the first medieval pleasure carriage (the German *Kobelwagen*) and by early modern times both tilt-carts and tilt-wagons played a continuous and ubiquitous rôle: illustrations of them as passenger vehicles from sixteenth-century Germany or England (a woodcut for Spenser's *Shepheards Calendar* of 1581) and they were very much a part of the English rural scene of the nineteenth century.[26] In North America the covered wagon became part of the history and myth of the westwards expansion, where from the 1750s the renowned Conestoga Wagon, first built in Lancaster county, Pennsylvania, from English and German prototypes, was a 4-m long tilt-wagon.

The medieval covered pleasure carriage

As we turn to the prestige pleasure carriages of the Middle Ages (an amenity for which we shall see society was primarily indebted to aristocratic ladies, supported by the higher clergy), we have once again to depend on iconographic and textual evidence in default of surviving vehicles before the fifteenth and sixteenth centuries. The lexical evidence is at first in Latin, the lingua franca of the literate cleric, civil servant or diplomat of Italy or France, Germany or England. The vehicle vocabulary is by no means free of ambiguities (as in the original classical Latin), and the equation of name and technological type not always easy or certain. In general in the early Middle Ages classical vehicle names were used especially in literary or poetical exercises where the writer may be showing off his learning: we saw Einhard in the ninth century, aiming at a Suetonian style, used *carpentum* of the ceremonial ox-carts of the Merovingian kings, and when a German saint's life of 1150 speaks of merchants *cum carpentis* we may suspect tilt-carts as at Roman Klagenfurt, but with no certainty. On the Continent, by the full Middle Ages, usage seems on the whole to have settled down to *biga* or *careta* for a two-wheeled cart, *carrus* or *plaustrum* for a four-wheeled wagon.[27] But in England Langdon's invaluable survey from manorial accounts, 1250–1420, shows the three most common types were two-wheeled carts called *plaustra*, *carecta* and *carra* (he gives good reason for regarding *plaustrum* as a two-wheeled ox-cart) and four-wheelers known as *carrus* or *currus* – 'clearly not farm vehicles but showy household conveyances'. These are the vehicles we are seeking; on the English medieval farm all transport was by varieties of two-

wheeled carts drawn by oxen or horses in view of the virtual
impossibility of manoeuvring fixed-axled four-wheelers: 'wagons
were virtually non-existent on farms until at least the seventeenth
century'.[28] The variants *carra* and *caretta* were further differentiated,
from the thirteenth century, as short and long – *curta* or *longa*, cart
or carriage.

In the Viking world of the early ninth century, the panel of
embroidery from the famous Oseberg ship-burial in Norway shows
two types of horse-drawn vehicle with four solid disc wheels,
one an open car with driver and passenger, and the others very
conventionalized tilt-covered carriages.[29] In his study of the medieval
suspended coach body, a peculiar type to which we will return, Lynn
White drew attention to an Arabic text of *c*.965, the account of the
Spanish Jew, Ibrahim ibn Ya'qub, of his travels among the western
Slavs, who reported, 'Their kings ride in big, rumbling, high vehicles
with four wheels, and with four sturdy poles at the corners from
which a brocade-covered *haudaj* is suspended by strong chains so
that whoever sits in it does not feel the jolting.' *Haudaj* is glossed
by another Arabic writer of 1311 as 'a conveyance for
women...roofed over by arched wood', and as *howdah* became
familiar to the British Raj as a canopied seat on an elephant. So by
the tenth century, at least in north and northeast Europe we have
evidence for high-status four-wheeled carriages which could be tilt-
covered, appropriate to royalty, and perhaps with a hint of women
passengers as well.[30]

Coming now to the main body of our evidence in Europe and
England from the twelfth century, for the first carriages for parade
and pleasure, we must remember that a documentary reference to a
carrus does not in itself indicate whether an open or closed vehicle
is in question. To anticipate, the iconography of passenger vehicles is
almost exclusively for tilt-covered carriages, but we may conveniently
start with a twelfth-century open carriage. The drawings in Herrad
of Landsberg's *Hortus deliciarum* of *c*.1170 are known to us only
from early nineteenth-century copies, the original manuscript at
Strasbourg being burnt in the Franco-Prussian war of 1870. Among
the allegorical illustrations are three of vehicles, two 'chariots' with
two wheels, and one four-wheeled carriage. The artist combines an
odd mixture of conventionalism and accurate detail: the two-wheelers
and their horse-teams, *Pharao* and *Auriga*, and *Sol* with *Equi solis*,
are simply square boxes, but the latter is well known as the earliest
depiction of harnessing with the whipple-tree, shown in detail. The

long open carriage with low gaily painted sides leaves us in no doubt
of its name and status, for it is titled *Gemmatus currus luxurie*, The
Glittering Carriage of Wantonness. In it the artist has packed sixteen
passengers with their names, headed by *Luxuria* herself, scattering
flowers. Behind her are fifteen armoured knights led by *Amor*,
bearing Cupid's bow, followed by fourteen others: this sorry crew
are the Seven Major and Seven Minor Vices, duly labelled *Pompa*,
Turpitudo, *Fornicatio* and so on. This amusingly disreputable scene
appears to be the only representation of an open *currus*. Boyer noted
the implausibility of its harnessing to a pair of horses by ropes, but
it may be noted that these are shown attached not to the body of
the carriage but to its front axle, and so allowing for an interpretation
of pivoting, with some degree of locking in turning.[31]

White drew attention to an early eleventh-century English manuscript with drawings of the same unique type of passenger vehicle,
an uncovered hammock-type fabric or leather body suspended from
four corner-posts on a four-wheeled undercarriage, one at least
carrying Joseph in Pharaoh's second-best chariot. The drawings are
very schematic, some clearly unfinished, and all suggest the artist
working from a verbal description rather than the real object.
By the early fourteenth century an accomplished illuminator is
portraying, clearly from life, a similarly suspended body of wickerwork, packed with the six wives of Jacob's sons, part of the family's
move to join Joseph in Egypt, the whole under a barrel-vaulted tilt
of what was by that time a standard form.

I would make some points on the slung body of passenger carriages
not noted by White. In the first place it was a conscious attempt,
however clumsy, to achieve some comfort in four-wheeled vehicles
without springs, and as such presupposes an appreciable period of
discomfort before its record among the western Slavs in the tenth
century or Anglo-Saxon England in the eleventh. Here we may
properly take account of an alternative means of transport, especially
for ladies or royalty in medieval and early modern times: the litter
carried between two horses on lateral poles. King John is described
as travelling *in lectica equestri* by a fifteenth-century chronicler;
covered litters with female passengers are shown in fourteenth-
century manuscripts, and John Leland, writing of the bridal procession of the princess Margaret Tudor to James IV of Scotland in
1503, records not only 'a char richly drest, with six faire horsys' but
'one very riche litere borne by two faire coursers vary nobly drest'.
('Char' as we shall see was used for a carriage from Chaucer

onwards.) Litters continued to be used for sick persons up to the seventeenth century – John Evelyn shared a litter with his invalid father in September 1640, and its modern descendant is the hospital stretcher.[32] Four-point suspension continued in coach design until the use of effective steel springs in the late eighteenth century, as we shall see. A final point is that these early carriages already had a hint, in the *haudaj* of the Slav carriage, of an association with women passengers, confirmed by medieval iconography where women are consistently shown in covered long carriages. I would suggest that the initiative and precursors of the coach as a closed travelling vehicle came not from the kings and knights, but from the aristocratic ladies of the court and noble families, aided and abetted by the higher clergy and all in search of such comfort as could be gained when on wheels. Comfort and protection from the weather, the dust and mud: it may be no coincidence that the thirteenth and fourteenth centuries saw an elaboration and a new richness in women's dress simultaneously with the developed closed carriage.

Our earliest explicit account of closed carriages as a part of royal display comes from the twelfth century and a writer already known to the reader, William Fitzstephen with his interest in horses. He was a member of the entourage of Thomas Becket, whose life he wrote and whose murder he witnessed in Canterbury Cathedral in 1170. In 1158, when Becket was Archdeacon of Canterbury and Chancellor of England under Henry II, at that time on terms of close friendship, the Chancellor led an embassy to the court of the French king Louis VII to seek the betrothal of Henry's eldest son to Margaret, Louis's daughter. Fitzstephen was one of Becket's attendants and wrote at first hand. They were out to make a great show – *parat ostendere et effundere luxus opulentiam* – taking with them twenty-four changes of raiment; silks, miniver and ermine, some 200 horses for Becket's household; dogs and hawks as gifts. More important were eight state carriages, *octo bigas curules*, with iron-shod wheels, and tilts of stitched leather, *bigae ferratae, magnis coriis animalium consutis coopertae*. Each was drawn by a team of five horses of destrier standard, *quinque equi trahebant, dextrariis corpore et robere similes*. Two of them carried a special gift to the French king, iron-hooped casks of a particularly fine brew of ale (the appropriate English drink to wine-drinking France), one was the Chancellor's private room (*camera*), another his chapel (*capella*), another his kitchen; the remainder held food and drink, bedclothes, carpets and curtains in sacks and bags. The clergy and attendant gentry rode on horseback. This great diplomatic mission crossed the Channel in what must have been a flotilla of ships, sailing up the Seine to Meulan (Seine-et-Oise) and then on land to Paris through Lagny, Corbeil, Pontoise and St Denys with provisions supplied on the way by command of the king: *panes et carnes et pisces, vina et cibaria in abundantia.* When they entered Paris the great carriages with their iron-shod wheels creaked and rattled over the paving stones, *stridebant ad platearum.*[33]

Here then we have carriages, four-wheeled with leather-covered tilts drawn by teams of five powerful horses (in line, as we shall see), used in a display of regal magnificence for transport of goods and for accommodation at least when at rest, and a point of nomenclature arises: Fitzstephen does not use the term of *currus* or *carrus*, but *biga, bigas curules, bigae ferratae*, in classical Latin a two-horsed vehicle of chariot type and in medieval Europe, as Haupt noted, a two-wheeled cart. Clearly Becket's vehicles were heavy four-wheeled covered wagons, and here Fitzstephen is once again the conscious stylist using classical diction, inventing a phrase, *bigas curules* for the carriages of plenipotentiaries (and perhaps with another Vergilian echo in their screeching noise)[34] and disdaining the current English vernacular Latin usage. His contemporary William of Malmesbury, another writer of stylish Latin, again turned to the classical vocabulary when he termed the vehicle in which William Rufus's corpse was taken from the New Forest as *rheda caballaria,*[35] a horse-drawn four-wheeler, as *raeda* properly denoted. A comparable appearance of covered carriages following the mounted nobility is quoted from a German account of the emperor Henry VII in 1312–13, with a hoop-tilted *Kobelwagen* covered with leather or fabric for the ladies of the court, a *Kammerwagen* with beds, baggage, table-ware, tents, cushions, rugs etc., and a *Kappelwagen* with altar, altar-cloths, shrines and the sacred vessels.[36]

John Langdon has quoted examples of carriages in the households of the higher clergy at this time. In the property of the Bishop of London in 1303 appears *uno carro cum apparatu pro quinque equis*; of the Bishop of Exeter in 1310 *j carro cum iiij rotis*. Better still, a Yorkshire canon owned *j karr cum iiij rotis et v fallaris de nigro pro v equis, ad trahendum hujus modi currum*, five horses with black cloth trappings. Clearly a five-horse team goes with a four-wheeled carriage, leaving little doubt of the nature of Becket's *bigas curules*. There is scope for further work by historians and students of vehicle technology on the documents: James Willard's papers on land transport in England are now over sixty years old, and he did not quote the original Latin of his numerous references to carts and wagons, rendering their identification uncertain.[37]

I have left for consideration the iconographic evidence for the closed carriage from the fourteenth century until early modern times. To my knowledge it comprises some half-a-dozen representations between *c*.1350 and 1450 in manuscript and other paintings and one embroidery, and from 1451 and 1526 actual body frames. Other examples may well exist unpublished or obscurely recorded. By the later sixteenth century actual carriages survive, such as the bridal car of the Princess Dorothea of Denmark, 1560–61, or the carriages at Coburg of 1560 and 1584.[38] The available evidence is consistent for a long four-wheeled carriage with an arched tilt of leather or fabric over a bent-wood hooped frame, forming a 'barrel-vaulted' structure of inverted ∩ or omega Ω section. Both types are extremely ancient, going back to the surviving mid second-millennium BC ox-wagons in the Caucasus, though there is no necessary continuity between members of so technically simple a construction. Perhaps, however, in the west we may go back to Roman times and the *carpentum*, if that in fact is the name of the vehicle with arched tilt shown for instance on the Agrippina coins, mentioned earlier on. What we know of it was that it was two-wheeled, the tilt richly decorated, and it was used for privileged women: something similar might also have been used by the Merovingian kings.

We may begin our iconographic survey by going back to Lynn White's paper on the slung or suspended carriage-body and its illustration from a manuscript of Rudolph of Ems's World Chronicle of 1330–1350 of a suspended and tilt-covered carriage, shown in great detail, conveying Jacob's daughters-in-law to Egypt. From an earlier manuscript (but after *c*.1300) Haupt published another version of the same scene, showing a rather schematic two-wheeled cart, packed with women under a stylized canopy:[39] White's later version is of a four-wheeled carriage shown in detail, drawn by a pair of horses harnessed by collars and traces to a central draught-pole. The passenger body is of shallow basket-work, slung at the four corners to uprights of the undercarriage, with a U-shaped hooped tilt carried on five arched members joined by six longitudinal rods and covered with a fabric cover partly rolled back to show the six ladies of Jacob's family. Continuing with fourteenth-century Continental examples, an embroidered coffin pall from the Ebsdorf monastery in Saxony of the second half of the century shows a four-wheeler with a tilt and a row of women, taken to be the children of Israel crossing the Red Sea. A French manuscript of *c*.1317, a life of St-Denis, shows again a four-wheeled carriage drawn by at least two horses in line, with shafts and traces and an arched tilt, with the lateral rods of the frame ending in decorative knobs at each end, and five women passengers looking out of the windows of the covering. Another similar carriage appears in the Toggenburg Bible of 1411, again showing Jacob and his family travelling to Egypt. Continental examples continue with a panel painting of *c*.1430 at Lübeck, showing St Elizabeth of Hungary conveyed with other ladies in an identical four-wheeled carriage with a tilt probably of leather, with decorative knobs to the frame rods and a single window. One trace-harnessed horse of the draught team is shown. A Jean le Tavernier miniature in Brussels of 1455 shows a single lady in a narrow-bodied open-sided country wagon with omega-framed tilt over which a crimson cloth has been loosely thrown, drawn by shaft- and trace-harnessed horses and has on the whole an air of informality alien to the other formal carriages. A 1470 Froissart manuscript shows again what is now a standard type.[40]

But by far the most splendid portrayal of the tilt-covered long carriage for aristocratic ladies is English, contained in the famous Psalter written and illuminated for Sir Geoffrey Luttrell of Irnham in Lincolnshire in 1320–40. Here, in a double-spread coloured drawing occupying the lower margins of two folios, is a particularly magnificent carriage with its full team of five horses in line, a Group *pl. 13* of Noble Dames as passengers, their attendants and their pets. This is no sober scene from hagiography or Holy Writ, but a picture of elegant frivolity in high places. The carriage has four six-spoked tyred wheels, the sides of the body painted with repeated heraldic panels, *azure a double headed eagle displayed or*, under a cusped arcading. It is open at both ends, the sides flanked by grotesque bird-caryatids, and a gilded chain slung across at each end. The U-shaped tilt has the knobbed ends of the lateral rods turned into gargoyle-heads and is covered with red leather decorated with gold arabesques; two rolled-back panels make a pair of windows (no doubt repeated on the other side) from which two ladies look out. The passengers are four ladies in coronets, the one in front with a pet squirrel nibbling a nut on her shoulder, and her companion at the rear is having her lap-dog handed her by a servant. The five-horse team, harnessed in tandem, comprises three piebalds and two bays, the last of which, between shafts, carries a rider with a very long whip,

16 Covered carriage with women passengers,
from the Toggenburg Bible, 1411.

and the second horse of the remainder of the trace-harnessed team
has also a rider.[41]

The Luttrell carriage entirely conforms with, and amplifies, all the
details of the other less precise representations and the texts, but
raises its own problems. Marjorie Boyer was worried that the
harnessing betweeen shafts that prolong the undercarriage, like those
of a cart, would preclude a pivoted front axle and so might be a
convention rather than the depiction of a long vehicle incapable of
even a degree of lock in turning. But a striking feature of the Luttrell
genre scenes is an (admittedly subjective) impression of a portrayal
of actuality in personal detail, like the family dinner-party with the
girls in dresses of more up-to-date fashion than their mother;
other genre scenes, with two accurately rendered carts and the
individualized faces of the labourers, suggest observation on the
manor farm: even if one cart is driven by a monkey this could be a
family joke – a carter known as Old Monkey-Face. I feel the great
carriage should be accepted as a literal portrayal of a four-wheeler
with two fixed axles incapable of turning without a controlled skid
and the same seems to be the case with the Toggenburg Bible vehicle.
The price of prestige and the honouring of ceremonial convention
can outweigh convenience and commonsense, from the prehistoric
fixed-axled ox-wagons of the Ukraine or the Pazyryk carriage, to
the absurd archaic inconvenience of the Royal Coaches or the Lord
Mayor's Coach of today. The surviving Elizabethan royal coach in
the Kremlin, which we shall encounter later, has such a limited lock
that a turning circle of 35 m (120 ft) has been estimated for it (as
against the 8.5 m of Hallstatt).

I would go further and suggest we might estimate approximate
measurements for the Luttrell carriage on the assumption that the
drawing is very roughly to scale. Taking the horses on Fitzstephen's
authority for such a team to be of destrier stature, we could take a
withers height of about 150 cm as a module. Using this we would
obtain a length for the carriage of some 5 m (16 ft) and a height of
1.85 m (6 ft) from the floor to the apex of the tilt, with 1.5 m diameter
wheels. Width is wholly conjectural, but recent wagon shafts give
0.9 m (3 ft) clearance for a cart-horse, and the medieval horse may
have needed less. With decreasing certainty we can guess the length
of the five-horse team as about 15 m (50 ft) and so, to return to
Becket's cavalcade of 1158, the eight carriages and their horses in
line could have stretched for something like 185 m – a furlong, an
eighth of a mile. My figures are speculative, but give a fair general

impression. Where the Luttrell artist saw his carriage is unknown, but it has been suggested that it might have been on the Great North Road near the Luttrell estates, and hardly in the local lanes.

By the middle of the fifteenth century we have a surviving wooden body and tilt framework, but no undercarriage or wheels, from the bridal carriage of Frederick III and the Infanta Eleanor of Portugal of 1451. This elaborately carved piece is comparable to another surviving body of a bridal carriage, that of the Princess Sibyl of Saxony of 1526, and those of 1549 and 1572 in the Palazzo Serego-Alighieri at Verona, where ·the final bosses of the lateral framing rods are carved with human masks like the Luttrell ones.[42] These sixteenth-century tilts are all of omega section and recall the modern Bow-top and Open-lot romantically 'traditional' English gypsy caravan – traditional only from the 1850s, when gypsies adapted the living-van from the travelling showmen.[43] The sixteenth-century ceremonial tilt carriages were to be the last of the line of long covered carriages going back at least to the twelfth century and continuing as the vehicle especially favoured by aristocratic ladies for some three centuries. But the long carriage with arched tilt was to be a dead end in coach design. From the sixteenth century new types of body were invented, and the tilt-wagon slipped down the social scale.

From tilt-carriage to coach

The new developments took place in Germany, the Low Countries and northeast France, part of the traditional wagon country of continental Europe: England, part of the cart zone of the Atlantic coasts, was a backwater. The Luttrell carriage, with no mitigation against discomfort and jolting, is contemporary with that of the Rudolph of Ems Chronicle, with the sophistication of a slung body; Luttrell too retains shaft-harnessing with its incapability of a locking turn. With the end of the *caretta longa*, English transport at the level of the court and high fashion looked to Europe for refinement and increased if still relative comfort and lightness. There too the carriage was changing its social status from Women's Carriage to Everyone's Carriage, even if in the sixteenth-century court of Charles IX of France there were mutterings of *effemination asiatique* in the manner of Aubrey in England a century later.[44]

Vocabulary is as so often revealing. In the Romance languages a cognate series from the *currus, carra, caretta* roots developed; in

French usage the modern *char* for the two-wheeled chariot of antiquity, and *chariot* or *charette* for a farm wagon evolved. In English on the other hand, while medieval Latin for cart was *carecta* a parallel sequence for a carriage or state car, as in Chaucer at the end of the fourteenth century, starts with 'char' ('With laurer crouned, in his char gold-bete') and goes on as 'chare' in for instance the ballad of *The Sqyr of Lowe Degree* of *c.*1475, and John Skelton at the end of the century ('goodly chares'). By the 1580s Renaissance scholars translating the classics turned to 'charet' for the words used for chariots – Sir Henry Savile in his Tacitus of 1591 – but quickly 'chariot' came in – Sir Clement Edmonds translating Caesar in 1604. The Authorized Version of the Bible of 1611 has 'charet' in its first printing, 'chariot' in all subsequent editions: Cotgrave in his French-English dictionary of 1611 glosses French *chariot* as 'wagon'. Then, by the time of Pepys and onwards, a 'chariot' in contemporary usage was a light private four-wheeled coach; in a novel of 1796 an antiquarian parson 'rode sometimes out in his chariot', and by 1801 one could speak characteristically of a 'genteel chariot'.[45]

The Germanic languages chose to use another line of Indo-European derivatives, from the *vegh*-root, as in Latin *vehiculum*. From Old English this gives early Modern English 'wain', which Langdon has shown equates in farming terms with the medieval ox-drawn, two-wheeled *plaustrum*. 'Wain' begins to be used from the sixteenth century, whereas the four-wheeled horse-drawn 'wagon' was not established in cart-zone England until it was adopted, probably from the Low Countries, in the seventeenth century, from the general European wagon-zone.[46] In German, *Wagen* provides an all-purpose vehicle word qualified by infinite compounds, as *Streitwagen* for a war chariot, *Lastwagen* as a heavy-duty four-wheeler (today a truck or lorry), and in passenger vehicles *Kobelwagen* for a tilt-wagon or carriage and *Kastenwagen* for an early coach: *Kobel* is a dovecot (presupposing a vernacular barrel-roofed pigeon loft) and *Kasten* a box. It was this last, the closed box-like body with a four-wheeled undercarriage, which won the day as the tilt-carriage lost social status at the end of the sixteenth century. The term 'coach' itself seems, with reason rather than romance, to come from the Hungarian village of Kocs, on the Budapest–Vienna main road, and has been associated with the king Matthias Corvinus (1458–90). Tarr has discussed the complicated evidence for late fifteenth-century passenger carriages called *kocsi* in Latin, Italian, German, French, English and other linguistic variants.[47] From this point onwards we are justified in using the generalized word 'coach' for the wide variety of prestige pleasure carriages that proliferated from the sixteenth century to the nineteenth. It is not my purpose in this essay to attempt a technological and social history of the coach: much has been done though much, particularly in accurate vehicle technology, still remains to be done. All I shall do is to sum up a few salient points so far as they concern the early development of the prestige vehicle that became a focus of vanity, display and ostentation in early modern Europe as a gratification psychologically identical to that of the expensive motor-car of today.

The technological problem facing the early coach-builders was the provision of comfort and shelter in travel, however limited, above all by reducing jolting and vibration by some form of springing, and a general reduction of the body weight. This was not finally resolved until the supply of high-grade tensile steel to make either laminated and elliptical or semi-elliptical leaf springs between body and undercarriage, or massive C-springs for its suspension. The former were known as early as 1615–16, and the latter again in the seventeenth century, but both had to wait general adoption for a century.[48] The basic springing principle of the first coaches was that of suspension by metal chains or leather straps from the four lower corners of the box-body to uprights set on the undercarriage in the manner traced by Lynn White for the medieval tilt-carriages in fourteenth- and fifteenth-century Germany and the Low Countries, as we saw earlier. And other constructional features may have played their part. If, as we look at the Danish Princess Dorothea's bridal carriage of 1560, we think not wholly seriously of a pretty little Baroque four-poster bed on wheels, we may not be far wrong. The open canopied body is in fact the equivalent of the bed with its tester, posts and curtains, as a sheltered refuge on a litter out-of-doors no less than in a chilly and draughty great bedroom.

In following the use of prestige pleasure carriages in the west from early modern times, the evidence available naturally increases exponentially with the direct records of the now specialized coach-builders and the survival of their products; the spread of printing, woodcuts and metal engraving and other pictorial records; the torrent of literary and historical allusions. I shall therefore confine myself to England, as an interesting case of indigenous tradition absorbing extraneous innovation, and within this area touch only on a few instances of that recurrent motif of antiquity, the interchange or gift of prestige objects by potentates. What at the time was seen as the problem of 'the first coach in England' engaged the antiquaries from the end of the eighteenth century, and can now be seen to have arisen partly in a confusion of technological and lexical terms.[49] The long covered carriage of Luttrell type continued in aristocratic use well into the sixteenth century for the conveyance of ladies (as in the coronation of Henry VIII in 1509 and Elizabeth herself in 1558) as well as for baggage and household goods in noble families. What was new was the box-carriage slung or directly mounted on wheels, the coach, which as we saw was a continental invention and not part of the indigenous English tradition of carriage design. It was seen by contemporaries as an alien innovation to be set precisely in the 1550s. The redoubtable Elizabethan antiquary John Stow, who died in 1605, recorded in his *Annales* under the year 1555, 'This yeare Walter Rippon made a coche for the Earl of Rutland, which was the first coche that ever was made in England.' Henry, the second Earl of Rutland, had accompanied the 1551 embassy to Henri II of France to arrange for the betrothal of Edward VI to his daughter, and may have encountered continental coaches at that time; he was later to become a favourite of Queen Elizabeth. Stow goes on, '*in anno* 1564 the said Walter Rippon made the first hollow turning coche for Her Majesty, being then her servant'.[50] The distinguishing features of this vehicle were evidently that it was not only covered ('hollow') but that it could turn with a pivoted front axle, unlike the rigid-axle tilt-carriage of Luttrell type. It is not surprising that the Queen's first coachman should be a Dutchman, William Boonen, as new skills of driving a mobile four-wheeler with a pair of horses were needed, quite unlike the fixed-track long carriage with a five-horse in tandem.

Elizabeth attended the opening of Parliament in 1571 in such a new-fangled coach driven by Boonen, and further information on the Queen's transport comes in a letter from the English ambassador at the French court of Henri III, to Elizabeth in 1582. 'The French King', he writes,

hath commanded to be made for your Majesty an exceeding marvellous princely coche, and to be provided foure of the fairest moiles [mules] which are to be had, for to carry your Highness's litter. The king has been moved to show himself in this sort, grateful to your Majesty on receiving those dogs and other singularities which you lately pleased to send unto him for his falconer.[51]

This passage is full of interest. In the first place it records an act of ceremonial gift-exchange between monarchs of the type we have encountered throughout antiquity, including domestic animals and prestige vehicles as in Akkadian Mesopotamia or Zhou China, or animals alone as Charlemagne's Spanish horses given to the Islamic embassy in 807, or Pope Benedict XII's Great Horse sent to China in 1340. In 1582 Henri III sent mules for the royal litter still in use; these animals with their Mediterranean ancestry were appropriately French and Elizabeth had sent hawks and hounds, as had Henry II to Louis VII in 1158. By early modern times domestic dogs had fully acquired their own social ranking appropriate to that of their owners, with hunting dogs at the top; as the Mayor of Liverpool put it in 1567, 'greyhounds, hounds and spaniels, that is gentlemen's dogs'.[52] The Elizabethan Englishman was proud of his breeds of hounds, and with some historical warrant. The quality of British hunting dogs was known to the classical world of Pliny and Strabo; Irish wolf-hounds were valued in Rome at the time of Symmachus at the end of the fourth century (the date of the fine bronze votive model from the Nodons shrine at Lydney in Gloucestershire), and were sent by Archibishop Ussher, Primate of Ireland, as a gift to Cardinal Richelieu in 1640.[53] In 1582 Henri III trumped Elizabeth's card by the gift of the most up-to-date piece of continental travel-technology, a coach. It is the wry irony of history that it was in the French royal coach that the king's successor, Henri IV, would be assassinated in the Paris streets in 1610.

The coach accepted

In the long history of the acceptance or rejection by a society of technological innovations, the immediate and enthusiastic adoption in England of the new coach as a prestige vehicle from the Continent is a classic example. The temper of the times was exactly right. By the sixteenth century England was in a mood not only of national self-confidence, but sharing the pride of the Renaissance conviction that the Moderns could not only equal but surpass the Ancients in technology. A new age was at hand, not only in the reformed churches but in the secular emancipation of knowledge and its practical application; Bacon's Great Instauration and Experiments not only Luciferous but Fructiferous, advancing pure science and applying it, technology for man's use such as printing, the magnetic compass and gunpowder. The millenarians were excitedly quoting the prophet Daniel, 'many shall run to and fro, and knowledge shall be increased', and saw foreshadowed the new voyages of discovery:

mobility and travel could be increased by better coaches too. Prestige as we have seen throughout antiquity has its price, in transport as in any display of ostentation to achieve status, but snobbery is always prepared to pay. In Elizabethan England there was New Money around with the prosperity of the rising merchant class especially in London and the big towns, and parading an expensive vehicle as a demonstration of affluence is an affectation still very much with us today.

In London coaches quickly moved from a fashion to a craze. By 1601 a Bill was laid before Parliament 'to restrain the excessive use of coaches'. John Taylor, with a vested interest as a waterman on the Thames, in 1623 wrote of the 'needless, vpstart, fantasticall and time-troubling' coaches, of 'vpstart four-wheeled tortoises' 'damming up the streetes and lanes': 'This is the rattling, roaring, rumbling age, and *The World runnes on Wheeles*'. Traffic jams built up in the medieval streets fit only for horse and foot passengers, until the coaches were 'like mutton pies in a cook's oven, hardly can you thrust a pole between', said Henry Peacham in 1636.

> How many paltry, foolish, painted things
> That now in coaches trouble every street
> Shall be forgotten

sighed the poet Michael Drayton as early as 1594.[54] And not only the citizens but the court. In 1600 four coaches of the embassy to Morocco and eight of that for Russia paraded the streets, and three years later the French embassy attending the accession of James I brought no fewer than 30 coaches with it.

A technical peculiarity of the seating arrangements in the first coaches noted by the contemporary pamphleteers and seen in iconography, was the provision of a seat facing outwards at each door, known as the 'boot'. These were normally occupied by women, who were in fact sitting back-to-back in contemporary side-saddle manner without stirrups on what were in effect the steps of the coach, with the door often hardly more than a framed leather apron, the whole not unlike a large boot in shape. Taylor laughed at this – 'it makes people imitate sea Crabs, in being drawne sidewayes, as they are when they sit in the Boote of the Coach.' The satirical Thomas Dekker in his *Guls Hornebooke* of 1609 makes the purpose clear: 'In the boots of which coach Lechery and Sloth sit like the Waiting-maid', ready to hand out her mistress down the side-saddle steps. The arrangement continued on women's coaches up to the end of the seventeenth century. By 1750 or so the 'boot' had become singular, and was applied to a box or locker at the rear of the coach, whence it has in turn become the modern motor-car boot.

The coach as prestige gift: Elizabeth and Russia

As we saw, by the 1580s coaches were taking a place as objects of high technology and craftsmanship suitable for diplomatic gift-exchange among the western nation-states of early modern Europe. As the mercantile and political networks extended, lands beyond the realms of Roman Christendom became regions where profitable trade and potential prestige might be sought and gained, and few more attractive in continental Europe than its eastern and alien neighbour, Russia. By the sixteenth century it was left as a giant anachronism, untouched by the Renaissance or humanistic thought, an archaic kingdom part a survivor of the ancient Near Eastern tradition, part Byzantine, cut off by its Slav language and since the tenth century by its literacy in the Old Church Slavonic script, from the Latinate west and its Roman tradition. English contacts virtually started with Richard Chancellor's accidental landing at the mouth of the river Dvina in 1553 and obtaining from the Tsar Ivan IV ('The Terrible') a tax-free trading monopoly confirmed as The Muscovy Company in two years' time. Thenceforward relations, commercial and political, were maintained between the two countries, an association always uneasy and potentially explosive in view of the xenophobia, arrogance and incompatible mores of both sides. As a part of the dignified haggling and jockeying for superiority was the interchange or at least presentation and acceptance of appropriately rich gifts.[55]

As a successor-state of the ancient oriental kingdoms, Russia not surprisingly preserved the customs of ceremonial gift-giving in their full form. As a Russian historian has recently written, 'During the sixteenth century an ambassadorial ritual was established in Russia, of which an important part was the presentation of diplomatic gifts.'[56] Of these gifts the most important were those in silver or gold, including many masterpieces of English Elizabethan and later dates, which were however valued not so much for their artistic qualities, as in a western European princely *Kunstkammer*,[57] but according to the more ancient classical or oriental scale of values, for their weight as bullion.[58] The Russian pieces each have their weights inscribed on them (in Old Church Slavonic) and a register was kept. An apt and early comparison from the ancient oriental world is the superb decorated silver bowls of Sassanian art of the third to sixth centuries AD with later (sixth- to seventh-century) inscriptions in Pahlavi and Sogdian recording their weights and ownership.[59]

But fine silver and silver-gilt vessels were not the only gifts from Elizabethan England accepted by the Tsar and still preserved today in the Moscow Kremlin Armoury Museum. There too is the earliest surviving English vehicle, a royal ceremonial coach of 1602–3, built as a diplomatic present and arriving with an ambassadorial party a few months after Elizabeth's death in March 1603. Coaches were no novelty to the Russian Court, as might be expected in the continental Wagon Zone, and as early as 1583, when Sir Jerome Bowes arrived as English Ambassador to the Tsar Ivan IV he records his journey to Moscow 'where mette me from the Emperour a Duke, well accompanied, which presented me a coch and tenne geldings'.[60] But this was not a royal gift between potentates at the highest level, and the 1603 coach was, as we shall see, a sumptuous affair of regal status.

The story of the embassy which brought it was chronicled by a member of the diplomatic entourage, published in 1605 and again by Samuel Purchas in *Purchas His Pilgrimes* of 1625, pruned 'where the censorious bitternesse also seemeth too much to insult' the Russian political scene.[61] The Elizabethan diplomatic presence in Moscow and often stormy relations with the Muscovy Company continued after the death of Ivan the Terrible in 1584 with Feodor and 1598 the election of the Tsar Boris Godunov, best known to most of us from Mussorgsky's opera. In September 1602 John Merrick returned to London from his Moscow tour of duty, and Sir Thomas Smith was appointed Ambassador in his place. But Elizabeth died in March 1603, and Sir Thomas did not sail from Gravesend until June, by that time as representative of James I. He arrived at Archangel on 22 June 1603 and made his way with his entourage and 'the great Present' for the Tsar, which included the ceremonial coach under discussion. The Ambassador travelled in his own coach, clearly now normal transport for one of his status: 'Then we did ride, til we came within a little mile of the many thousands of the Noblemen and Gentlemen on both sides of the way ... where the Embassadour alighted from his coach and mounted on his foot-cloth horse, and so rode on with his Trumpets sounding.' Then followed interminable ceremonial speeches from the Russian hosts, with a recital of their titles, honours, dominions and ranks ('Tedious Titles' Purchas comments in the margin), but finally 'we all presently mounted againe . . . the Ambassadour his horse and Foot-cloth being led by his page, some small distance, his Coach behind that'. The audience with Boris Godunov was on 11 October, Sir Thomas Smith 'having Iennets for himselfe, the King's Gentlemen, and good horses for the rest: as likewise two gallant white Palfreis to carry or draw a rich chariot, one parcell of the great Present.' Further items, we learn later, included 'thirtie yards of cloth of Gold and two standing Cups with covers' which survive today.[62] A vast feast for 200 was given, with an impressive display of plate, and strange food served on gold and silver dishes: they passed 'some foure houres in banquetting and refreshing ourselves too plentifully'. 'Garlike and Onions. Drinkes. Mead.' is Purchas's marginal note. By 15 October signs of an uprising under 'the false Dimitri' were apparent, but Smith and his embassy stayed over winter, had another audience with the Tsar and on 20 March 1604 'the Ambassador went from the Emperors sled to his coach set upon a sled and wee alighted from the Emperors horses, and betooke our selues to our easie and pleasant passage in sleds' to Archangel, where they took ship home on 28 May. Boris Godunov was to die suddenly (and perhaps suspiciously) the following April.

The English coach, the 'rich chariot, one parcell of the great Present' survives, as we have seen, in the Moscow Kremlin Armoury Museum today. We saw how around 1600 'chariot' was being used for a sumptuous state carriage, and the 1603 royal coach was a splendid piece of contemporary craftsmanship. Unfortunately it lacks publication beyond photographs in secondary sources, and a scale model commissioned in 1974 for the Science Museum, London, *pls. 14* where it is now housed, and of which two popular articles in obscure journals were published. No full description, measured drawings or technical description are yet available, and the following account has been pieced together from such evidence as is printed.[63]

The whole construction seems to be of oak, ironwork, leather and various velvets used in upholstery and curtains. Its undercarriage has a Y-shaped perch and a V-shaped draught pole, with a sway-bar pivoted to it at the front, as in traditional farm wagon design. Its wheel-base is 4.4 m (13 ft 2 in) and the gauge 1.65 m (5 ft 6 in) – within the normal range. It would have had a lock and turning circle of not less than 36.4 m (120 ft) in diameter. The elaborately carved wheels had twelve spokes: diameters are not recorded. The body is an open box with doors at each side and windows with curtains and leather 'boots'; glass was only being used tentatively from the end of the seventeenth century for coach windows. Indeed, the present royal Glass Coach, named in admiration of its large glass windows, was only added to the Royal Mews on King George V's coronation in 1910 (and so just within my own lifetime). The 1603 coach was of light boarding and leather on light curved posts, slung on uprights morticed to the undercarriage by leather straps covered in red velvet. The whole was adorned with elaborate gilded carved and painted panel enrichment, heraldic, decorative and pictorial, including scenes of Ivan IV's victory over the Tartars at Kazan in 1552, and hunting scenes and landscapes in the Dutch manner. Much fine gilded iron scroll work added opulence to what is indeed a 'rich chariot'. The present seating and upholstery of cut and uncut velvet seems to be of 1630–1660. The coach stands as the earliest surviving English carriage of magnificence, the next being the Gold State Coach of George III, built in 1762.[64]

The Indian Gift: James I and Jahangir

A second royal gift of a coach from a British monarch to a foreign potentate even more remote than Boris Godunov was made in 1615 by James I to the Grand Mogul, the emperor Jahangir of India (1605–27). This, nominally a present from king to emperor, was in fact sent at the instance and expense of the East India Company which, like the Muscovy Company but in far more bellicose conditions, was fighting its way against the Portuguese and to a lesser extent the Dutch to secure mercantile monopoly in India. Its eventual success and the establishment of the British Raj is a commonplace of history. In 1615 Sir Thomas Roe, an outstandingly able diplomat, was posted as Ambassador to the emperor Jahangir by James I to confirm and strengthen friendly relations between the two countries: he remained until 1618, having 'laid the foundation of British influence in India'. We are doubly fortunate in the extensive survival of his journals and letters, and in the recent publication of a first-class biography of Roe by Michael Strachan which fully documents the circumstances of the Jahangir episode.[65]

The Ambassador embarked for India on the newly-built *Lyon* on 2 February 1615, with his company including his chaplain, two musicians with virginals and trumpet to entertain the Great Mogul, and the former coachman of the Bishop of Coventry with a presentation coach as the main part of a diplomatic gift in the accepted manner. We saw in Chapter III in connection with the present of horses from England to Ranjit Singh in 1831 the value long placed in India on imported stock, but in the case of Jahangir local horses were evidently expected to be used, though the skill of an English coachman would be needed. It will be remembered how the Islamic world had come to reject the use and development of wheeled transport from an early date, and in Mogul India, despite the survival of an indigenous ox-cart tradition on a peasant level, a high-class horse-drawn carriage would be a novelty of the greatest rarity and esteem. Among the royal presents were hunting dogs in the manner of the day, mastiffs and Irish wolfhounds, and the dogs were a great success with the emperor. He eventually sent a reciprocal animal gift of antelopes to king James, two of which survived the journey home when Roe returned. By 23 September the *Lyon*, after an adventurous voyage, reached India and the embassy disembarked at Surat, the port near the mouth of the river Narbada north of Bombay, where it was allowed temporary residence en route to Jahangir's court, then at Ajmer, 400 miles NNE and 600 miles (965 km) by the route taken. The presentation coach was a nuisance, drawn by bullocks as a four-horse team had yet to be assembled and trained, and on its arrival at Ajmer it was pulled by hand into the emperor's presence to the accompaniment of music on the virginals. After the initial audience Jahangir commanded the musician and William Hemsell the coachman to remain behind and he himself 'got into the coach, into every corner, and caused it to be drawn about by them', as Roe reported. After this rather comic performance the coach was highly appreciated as an object of prestige, and with the traditional Indian skill in fine craftsmanship two replicas were soon built for the emperor. In November 1616 Roe saw and recorded the departure of Jahangir's son, prince Khurram, to command an army against Deccan, when the English coachman drove the prince in one of the two Indian copies, and later the emperor in the other, his queen Nur Mahal in the resplendently restored original. One wonders whether today in some forgotten dusty lumber room in an obscure palace a carriage may survive: in India almost anything is possible.

When Sir Thomas Roe was later Ambassador to the Ottoman Court in Constantinople he found himself again in the Islamic world of disregard for wheeled transport. Here there was no question of a diplomatic prestige gift, but in 1622 the grateful Levant Company, in whose interests he was then operating, sent him from England a replacement chaplain and a coach and coachman for himself and his wife. The coach was changing its status in England and becoming a less than princely index of worth, and more the symbol of high professional status. Roe may have had a coach in India where the adventurer Richard Steel was said to have 'lived in a style comparable to that of the Ambassador himself with a coach, palanquin, seven horses and ten servants'. Certainly in Constantinople the Levant Company felt it could enhance its prestige by providing its Ambassador with appropriate transport – indeed a company car.

Coaches to China: the great incompatibility

Our last instance of the British ceremonial presentation of a prestige vehicle to an alien monarch is the part of a disastrous failure of understanding between two incomprehensible and totally alien cultures. Indeed the Macartney Embassy from George III of Britain to the Manchu emperor of China, Qian-long, in 1793 is often quoted as a classic case of culture-clash between incompatible mores, with neither representative in the least capable of or attempting to an understanding of the other. It is well documented, and as in all misunderstandings, has an underlying element of inadvertent comedy.[66]

In 1793 George III informed the Celestial Emperor that he proposed to send an Ambassador Plenipotentiary and Extraordinary, Lord George Macartney, to present gifts to Qian-long on the occasion of his 83rd birthday. The mission in fact was wholly commercial in its purpose, to facilitate the Canton trade, notably in tea, while opening up new markets for British manufactures. Or at least so the British saw it, a political arrangement between two great powers on a more or less equal footing. But it could hardly be so for the holder of the Mandate of Heaven, whose Celestial Empire embraced the whole world, 'ruling all within the four seas', under which George III was a distant barbarian vassal. The emperor's reply is a superb piece of courteously condescending insults, opening 'We, by the Grace of Heaven, instruct the King of England to take note of our charge', going on to appreciate 'your sincere humility and obedience' but pointing out that the emperor 'does not value rare and precious things...we have never valued ingenious articles nor do we have the slightest need for your country's manufactures.' Macartney and George III were politely reminded that they were dealing with an ancient civilization with a long and distinguished history of inventive craftsmanship and technology.

The Ambassador Plenipotentiary arrived like a commercial representative with a full range of samples. These were not all trivial or irrelevant, for consultation had taken place in England in 1792 with two Chinese students from the College at Naples who were to act as interpreters to the Embassy, and who recommended scientific instruments, which would include a magnificent planetarium or Orrery made for the East India Company some years before, a barometer, an air-pump, terrestrial and celestial globes, a reflecting telescope and clocks by Vulliamy. It is however unlikely that Macartney knew of the Chinese Royal Observatories such as that on the Purple Mountain at Nanking with its great bronze equatorial instruments dating from AD 1276.[67] But more lightweight were the examples of English trade products such as glass chandeliers, Derby porcelain vases and figures, Birmingham swords and three coaches built by Hatchett of Long Acre. These last were hardly appropriate gifts to a civilization that had used pleasure carriages and Gentlemen's Chariots since the second millennium BC, and the more otiose since an English coach of 1782 required the coachman to sit in front of and at a higher level than the passenger, a clearly impossible position for the Celestial Emperor. The coaches eventually came to be stored away in the Royal Treasury of the Summer Palace to survive until the 1860s and its looting by the northern barbarians under Lord Elgin. The emperor Qian-long, who dabbled in the arts, summed up his view of the Embassy in a poem:

> Now England is paying homage
> My Ancestors' merit and virtue have reached their distant shore.
> Though their tribute is commonplace, my heart approves sincerely,
> Curios and the boasted ingenuity of their devices I prize not:
> Though what they bring is meagre, yes,
> In my kindness to men from afar I make generous return,
> Wanting to preserve my good health and power.

The end: the glamour of anachronism

By Macartney's time English coaches and carriages, in number, variety and acknowledged craftsmanship, were approaching the climax that they were to reach in the nineteenth century. From the accession of Queen Victoria onwards, members of the coach-builders' trade were writing as practical craftsmen and amateur historians of that subject: Adams in 1837, Thrupp twenty years later, and in America, Stratton in 1878.[68] 'Not many years back', wrote Adams, 'the varieties of carriage were very limited in number, and there was little room for the exhibition of taste in form. But this fault has of late been corrected, and the varieties of shape and make have become so numerous that it is difficult even for practical observers to be familiar with them all.' The abundant illustrations of 1820–1830 that make up the staple of popular histories of the carriage, often in varying degrees of sentimentality and nostalgia, confirm Adams's contemporary comment: we can here easily slip into the Christmas-card world of stage coaches in the snow. Adams, in his chapter of which the opening has just been quoted, goes on to describe some thirty types of carriage and illustrate half a dozen, and all the once-familiar names are there and their origins: the Barouche (from Germany about 1760), the Landau from Bavaria and the Britzschka from Austria, the Stanhope designed by the Honourable Fitzroy Stanhope in 1814 and the Tilbury named from his coach-builder, the Phaeton and the Cabriolet and the ubiquitous Gigs (which unaccountably moved Thomas Carlyle to an outburst of manic fury in his *French Revolution* published at this time). Later came the Hansom cab from its inventor (1834) and Lord Brougham and his coach (1839): royalty is involved with the Clarence (1840) and the Victoria (1867). By 1878 Stratton is listing and illustrating 50 English carriages, with another 60 from America. It has been estimated that by the 1850s nearly 400,000 carriages were in private use by the English upper and middle classes, 120,000 large four-wheelers and 250,000 smaller two-wheelers. Carriage and coach were the ubiquitous horse-drawn transport throughout society, the everyday conveyance of patrician and plebian, serving their solemn or trivial ends.

As a result of these social circumstances, prestige transport on great formal occasions was simply that of the everyday vehicles of life, differentiated only by the ostentation of the expensive coaches or carriages their owners could afford. As it happened, royal ceremonial from about 1800 became, as David Cannadine entertainingly showed, partly owing to the unpopularity of the ruling house, a shabby affair.[69] The last demonstration of magnificence in transport was the Royal Gold State Coach built for George III in 1762 at a *pl. 16* cost of £7,661, 'the most superb and expensive of any ever built in the kingdom': shortly before, in 1757, the coach for the Lord Mayor *pl. 17* of London had cost just over £1,000. The King's coach is a very fine and showy piece, lavishly gilded and with painted panels by Cipriani (to whom panels on the Lord Mayor's coach have also been attributed). Other royal coaches were the finer of the working vehicles in the Royal Mews, and if on occasion a procession was involved, peers and other guests came in their town coaches. But such occasions were few, scamped and sometimes disastrous in their ineptitude. The undertakers were drunk at Queen Charlotte's funeral in 1807; the coronations of George III and George IV were ceremonially incompetent; William IV walked out of George's funeral; at his own 'mourners loitered, laughed, gossipped and giggled'. Queen Victoria's coronation was unrehearsed and muddled by all officiating, including the Archbishop of Canterbury. Worse was to follow. The Queen, settling down to the rôle of dutiful and dowdy housewife, was no friend to flamboyant pageantry, and when after Albert's death in 1861, she took neurotic refuge in reclusive grief, the Widow of Windsor cast a further gloom over royal and ceremonial parade and the ostentation of its transport. Gladstone did not mince his words – 'the Queen is invisible and the Prince of Wales is not respected'.

Recovery of a proper sense of occasion and new respect for the throne was not any longer traditional, and a tradition had to be invented. This began with the Golden Jubilee of 1887 and set on its modern course by the Diamond Jubilee ten years later. By the end of the century the main complement of parade carriages in the Royal Mews were the splendid 1762 Gold State Coach (used in the coronations of both Victoria and Edward VII), the Irish State Coach bought by Victoria when it caught her fancy in the Dublin Exhibition of 1853, Queen Alexandra's Coach of 1893, the State Landau built for Edward VII in 1902, and the Glass Coach for George V in 1911. At George V's coronation most of the peers attended no longer in their coaches, but their motor-cars, a recently invented tradition of ceremonial transport; at the coronation of Queen Elizabeth II the extant stock of royal coaches had to be augmented by seven hired from a film company. The carriage of prestige for the ceremonial display of monarch and court survives today only as a nostalgic and now cherished archaism, preserved as an anachronism within the framework of a recently invented traditional past.

But custom and tradition, real or invented, have an endearing hold on the imagination. We saw how the English gypsies, having only adopted the travelling showman's living van in the 1850s, were burning it as a part of what by then was accepted as traditional funeral ritual in the 1950s: reports in the press suggest that motor vehicles are still burnt. But the last word on the ancient rite of vehicle burial, taking us back to the fourth millennium BC on the Russian Steppe and the ladies in their ox-wagons, comes appropriately enough from America and from Texas. On 19 May 1977 the widow of an oil millionaire, Mrs Sandra West of San Antonio, Texas, was buried sitting in her Ferrari motor car in a lace nightgown 'with the seat slanted comfortably'.[70]

Notes

Introduction (pp. 9–11)

1 J. Clutton-Brock, *Domesticated animals*, London 1981, 67–8.
2 For lions in early Greek literature and art, cf. T. Dunbabin, *Greeks and their eastern neighbours*, London 1957, 46; J. Boardman, *The Greeks overseas*, London & New York 1980, 78.
3 I owe this information to Mrs M.A. Littauer, quoting F.G. Roe, *The Indians and the horse*, Oklahoma University Press, 1955.

Chapter I (pp. 13–36)

1 A. Sherratt, 'Plough and pastoralism: aspects of the secondary products revolution', in I. Hodder *et al.* (edd), *Patterns of the Past: Studies in honour of David Clarke*, Cambridge 1981, 261–305.
2 M. Bloch, 'Technical change as a problem of collective psychology', in J.E. Anderson (trans. & ed), *Land and Work in Medieval Europe*, London 1967, 124–35.
3 S. Piggott, *Ancient Europe*, Edinburgh 1965, 17. Cf. A.M. Snodgrass, 'Conserving societies and independent development', in J.V.S. Megaw (ed), *To illustrate the monuments*, London & New York 1976, 58–62.
4 M.I. Finley, *The Ancient Economy*, Berkeley & Los Angeles 1973, 84.
5 R.W. Bulliet, *The camel and the wheel*, Cambridge Mass., 1975.
6 For all references not otherwise specified, S. Piggott, *The Earliest Wheeled Transport: from the Atlantic Coast to the Caspian Sea*, London & New York 1983, hereafter Piggott *EWT*.

7 M.A. Littauer & J. Crouwel, *Wheeled Vehicles and Ridden Animals in the Ancient Near East*, Leiden & Cologne 1979, 13–14.
8 E.Yu. Novitskiy, 'Derevjamnaya konstruktsiya ie yamnago pogrebeniya u sela Kholmskoe', *Sov. Arkh.*, 1982, 232–5.
9 For a splendid survey, R. Meiggs, *Trees and Timber in the Ancient Mediterranean World*, Oxford 1982.
10 R. Morgan, 'Studies at Haddenham', *Current Arch.* 118, 1990, 343–4.
11 Documentation to 1983 in Piggott, *EWT*; since then the main sources are: E. Woytowitsch, 'Der ersten Wagen der Schweiz, der ältesten Europas', *Helvetia Archaeologia* 61, 1985, 2–45; A. Sherratt, 'Two new finds of wooden wheels ...', *Oxford Journ. Arch.* 5, 1986, 243–53; A. Häusler, 'Neue Belege zur Geschichte von Rad und Wagen in nordpontischem Raum', *Ethnog.-Arch. Zeitschrift*, 25, 1984, 629–82; 'Rad und Wagen zwischen Europa und Asien', in W. Treue (ed) *Achse, Rad und Wagen*, Göttingen 1986, 139–52; G. Mansfeld, 'Gräber mit Wagenbeigaben vom ... Vorderen Asiens zur Hallstattzeit Europas', in M. Guštin & L. Pauli (edd) *Keltski Voz (Keltischer Wagengräber)*, Brezice 1984, 139–52.
12 M.A. Littauer & J.H. Crouwel, 'Early metal models of wagons from the Levant', *Levant* V, 1973, 102–26.
13 S. Piggott, 'Heads and Hoofs', *Antiq.* XXXVI, 1962, 110–18.
14 M.A. Littauer & J.H. Crouwel, 'Terracotta models as evidence for vehicles with tilts ...', *Proc. Prehist. Soc.* XL, 1974, 20–36.
15 S. Piggott, 'The earliest wheeled vehicles and the Caucasian evidence',

Proc. Prehist. Soc. XXXIV, 1968, 266–318.

16 Piggott, *EWT*, 83, 93, 98.

17 N.K. Sandars, *The Sea Peoples*, London & New York 1978, 120–24.

18 M. Ventris & J. Chadwick, *Documents in Mycenaean Greek*, Cambridge 1959, 211–13, 427.

19 Homeric horse-names, E. Delebecque, *Le cheval dans l'Iliade*, Paris 1957, 146.

20 Jean Ingelow (1820–1897), *High Tide on the Coast of Lincolnshire 1571*. The historical setting explains the archaistic 'uppe' but the scene is solidly Victorian.

21 Naming domestic animals: K. Thomas, *Man and the natural world*, London 1983, 96, 113–15.

22 Delebecque, *Le cheval ...*, 174–76; Piggott, *EWT*, 230.

23 N.J. Richardson & S. Piggott, 'Hesiod's wagon: text and technology', *Journ. Hellenic Stud.* CII, 1982, 225–9; H. Hayen, 'Zwei in Holz erhalten geleibene Reste von Wagenrädern aus Olympia', *Die Kunde*, NF 31/32, 1980/81, 135–91; Piggott, *EWT*, fig.78.

24 Piggott, *EWT*, 230–33.

25 K.D. White, *Farm equipment of the Roman world*, Cambridge 1975, 79–82; M.C. de Azevedo, *I trasporti e i traffico*, Rome 1938, 38–9.

26 J.C. Ginzrot, *Die Wagen und Fahrwerke der Griechen und Römer ...* Munich 1817; cf. A.C. Leighton, *Transport and communication in early medieval Europe*, Newton Abbot 1972, 96, 118.

27 Einhard, *Vita Caroli* (ed L. Halphen) Paris 1923; *Einhard and Notker the Stammerer: two lives of Charlemagne* (trans. & ed. L. Thorpe), Harmondsworth 1969.

28 Halphen, 10; J.M. Wallace-Hadrill, *The Barbarian West*, London 1952, 84; Thorpe, 181.

29 E.g. *Gaius* 15.1; *Claudius* 17.3; J.M.C. Toynbee, *Animals in Roman life and art*, London & New York 1973, 383, nn.140, 142.

30 Piggott, *EWT*, 231.

31 *Origines*, 20.12.4.

32 Toynbee, *Animals ...*, Pl.89; 186 and others similar, 383 n.141.

33 J. Werner, *Antiq.* XXXVIII, 1964, Pl.XXIX a.

34 M. Bloch, *Les rois thaumaturges*, London & Oxford 1924, 60–61.

35 Piggott, *EWT*, 225–8.

36 Measurements in G. Jenkins, *The English farm wagon*, Reading 1961, 218–25.

37 The facts are familiar, but concisely set out by J. Diamond, 'The gauge of British railways', *The Eagle* (St John's College Cambridge), LI, 1939, 240–48; cf. M. Robbins, *The Railway Age*, Harmondsworth 1970, 120.

Chapter II (pp. 37–68)

1 M.A. Littauer & J. Crouwel, *Wheeled Vehicles in ... the Ancient Near East*, 1979, 13–14; J. Zarins 'Equids associated with human burials in the third millennium BC', in R.H. Meadows & H.-P. Uerpmann (edd), *Equids in the Ancient World* (Wiesbaden 1986 (hereafter *Equids*)), 164–93.

2 C.P. Groves, 'Taxonomy, Distribution and Adaptation of recent Equids', in *Equids*, 11–65.

3 S. Bökönyi, *History of Domestic Mammals in Central and Eastern Europe*, Budapest 1974, 250–96; *The Przewalsky Horse*, London 1974; 'Horse' in I.L. Mason (ed), *Evolution of Domesticated Animals*, London & New York 1984, 162–73; J. Clutton-Brock, *Domesticated Animals*, London 1981, 80–90.

4 C.P. Groves in *Equids*, 11–65.

5 F.E. Zeuner, *A History of Domesticated Animals*, London 1963, 367–73.

6 J. Zarins, 'Equids associated with human burials ...', in *Equids*, 164–93; J.N. Postgate, 'The Equids of Sumer, again', *ibid.* 194–206; H. Behrens, *Die neolithischen-frümetalzeitlichen Tierskelettfunde der Alten Welt*, Berlin 1964, figs.9, 26, 27, 39; S. Piggott, 'Earliest

wheeled vehicles ...', *Proc. Prehist. Soc.* XXXIV, 1968, 307 (paired ox burials).
7 Littauer & Crouwel, *Wheeled Vehicles* ..., 1979, 28.
8 Lefebvre des Noettes, *L'Attelage et le cheval de selle* ..., Paris 1931; J. Spruytte, *Early Harness Systems*, London 1983.
9 For the lexical evidence, A. Salonen, 'Notes on wagons and chariots in ancient Mesopotamia', *Studia Orientalia* XIV, 2., 1950, 1–8; *Die Landfahrzeuge des alten Mesopotamien*, Helsinki 1951; *Hippologia Accadica*, Helsinki 1955; J. Zarins in *Equids*, 164–93; J.N. Postgate in *ibid.* 194–206.
10 Recent general surveys with references to sources in M.A. Littauer & J. Crouwel, *Wheeled Vehicles* ... 1979; J. Crouwel, *Chariots* ... *in Bronze Age Greece*, Amsterdam 1981; S. Piggott *EWT*, 1983, 109–37; P.R.S. Moorey, 'The emergence of the light, horse-drawn chariot in the Near East *c.*2000–1500 BC', *World Arch.* 18.2., 1986, 196–215; R. Drews, *The Coming of the Greeks*, Princeton 1988.
11 F. Hančar, *Das Pferd in prähistorischer und früher historischer Zeit*, Munich 1955; refs. in note 3 above; *Equids passim.*
12 D.Ya. Telegin, *Dereivka* (ed. J.P. Mallory), BAR Oxford, 1986; J.P. Mallory, *In Search of the Indo-Europeans*, London & New York 1989, 195–210; D.W. Anthony & D.R. Brown, 'The origins of horse-back riding', *Antiq*, 65, 1991, 22–38.
13 For the terrain, W. Brice, *South-West Asia*, London 1966, Chaps.7, 8; Kura-Araxes culture, S. Piggott, *Proc. Prehist. Soc.* XXXIV, 1968, 276–78; C. Burney & D.M. Lang, *The Peoples of the Hills*, London 1971, 75; F. Hančar, *Das Pferd* ... 162; A. Sagona, *Tell Aviv*, 8.2., 1981, 152–9 (radiocarbon dates); J. Zarins in *Equids*, 180.
14 S. Piggott, *EWT*, 88.
15 Often quoted: cf. A. Kammenhüber, *Hippologia Hethitica*, Wiesbaden 1961, 11.

16 S. Bökönyi, *Data on Iron Age horses in central and eastern Europe*, Cambridge Mass. 1968, 39.
17 J. Clutton-Brock, 'The Buhen horse', *Journ. Arch. Science* I, 1974, 89–100.
18 M.A. Littauer & J.M. Crouwel, *Chariots and related equipment from the tomb of Tut'ankhamūn*, Oxford 1985.
19 S. Piggott, *EWT*, 28.
20 J.E. Gordon, *Structures, or why things don't fall down*, Harmondsworth 1978, 145–6 (Mycenaean and Homeric).
21 M. Ventris & J. Chadwick, *Documents in Mycenaean Greek*, Cambridge 1959, 361–75.
22 M. Sparreboom, *Chariots in the Veda*, Leiden 1985, Chap. IV.
23 S. Piggott, 'Horse and chariot: the price of prestige', *Proc. Internat. Congress of Celtic Studies 1983*, Oxford 1986, 25–30.
24 Text, translation and commentary in A. Kammenhüber, *Hippologia Hethitica.*
25 M. Sparreboom, *Chariots in the Veda*, Chap.VIII (Glossary).
26 A. Kammenhüber, *Hippologia Hethitica*, 308–13. A. Dent, *The Horse through fifty centuries of civilization*, London 1974, 57, includes 'clover' but without warrant.
27 S. Piggott, 'Horse and chariot ...', 27.
28 W.P. Yetts, 'The horse: a factor in early Chinese history', *Eurasia Sept. Antiq.* IX, 1934, 232.
29 R. Drews, The *Coming of the Greeks*, 176.
30 Athenaeus XII, 528, quoted by Piggott, *EWT*, 133.
31 P.R.S. Moorey, 'The emergence of the light horse-drawn chariot ...', *World Arch.* 18.2, 1986, 196–215.
32 M.A. Littauer & J. Crouwel, *Wheeled Vehicles* ... 1979, 68, 99.
33 S. Piggott, *EWT* 1983, 27 and earlier papers of 1978–1979.
34 P.R.S. Moorey, *World Arch.* 18.2, 1986, 211.
35 J.P. Mallory, *In Search of the Indo-*

Europeans: Language, Archaeology and Myth, London & New York 1989, for all references save for those separately quoted.

36 S. Salonen, *Studia Orientalia*, XIV.2., 1950, 1–8; *Landfahrzeuge ...*, 1951.

37 R. Drews, *The Coming of the Greeks*, 1988.

38 Conveniently set out with references by M.S. Drower, 'Syria *c.*1550–1400 BC', *Camb. Anc. Hist.* Vol.II, Chap.X, Pt.1, Cambridge 1970; M. Mayrhofer, *Der Arier in vorderen Orient – ein Mythos?*, Vienna 1974 with valuable bibliography.

39 R.A. Crossland, 'Indo-European origins: the linguistic evidence', *Past and Present*, 12, 1957, 16–46.

40 J.P. Mallory, *In Search of the Indo-Europeans*, 1989, 41.

41 S. Piggott, *EWT*, 1983, 87–103; cf. W. Messerschmidt, 'Der agäische Streitwagen und zeine Beziehungen zum Nordeurasisch – vorderasiatischen Raum', *Acta Praehist. & Arch.* 20, 1988, 31–34 (ignoring *EWT*).

42 G.H. Mikaelian, *Cyclopean Fortresses in the basin of Lake Sevan*, Erevan 1968 (Armenian, English summary) and information in the field, 1966.

43 For a recent statement, A.F. Harding, *The Mycenaeans and Europe*, London 1984.

44 S. Piggott, *EWT*, 231–8.

45 A. Muzzolini, *L'Art rupestre préhistorique des massifs centraux Sahariens*, Oxford (BAR) 1986; 'Les chars ... du sudouest de la peninsule Ibérique ... les gravures rupestres du Maroc ... et la datation des chars Sahariens', *Actas Cong. Internat. Estrecho de Gibraltar*, Ceuta 1987, 361–87; S. Piggott, *EWT*, 131.

46 S. Piggott, *Prehistoric India*, Harmondsworth 1950, 276–281; S.D. Singh, *Ancient Indian Warfare with special reference to the Vedic period*, Leiden 1965; G. Margabandhu, 'Technology of transport vehicles in early India', in D.P. Agrawal & A. Gosh (edd) *Radiocarbon and Indian archaeology*, Bombay 1973,

182–89; M. Sparreboom, *Chariots in the Veda*, Leiden 1985.

47 M. Sparreboom, *Chariots in the Veda*, 5, 71.

48 A. Salonen, *Hippologia Accadica*, 208–47; R.T. O'Callaghan, 'New Light on the Maryannu as chariot-warrior', *Jahrb. für Kleinasiatischen Forsch.* I, 1951, 309–24.

49 A.R. Schulman, 'The Egyptian chariotry: a re-examination', *Journ. Amer. Research Center in Egypt* II, 1963, 75–98.

50 A. Salonen, *Hippologia Accadica*, 171.

51 Y. Yadin, *The art of warfare in Biblical lands*, London 1963, with fine illustrations.

52 Luidprand of Cremona, *Works* (trans. F.A. Wright), London 1930, 256–7.

53 Tutankhamun, Y. Yadin, *Art of warfare ...*, 214–215; Assurbanipal, H. Frankfort, *Art & Architecture of the Ancient Orient*, Harmondsworth 1954, Pls.108–12; Ras Shamra *ibid.* Pl.145.

54 Y. Yadin, *Art of warfare ...*, 284–7; P.R.S. Moorey, 'Pictorial evidence for the history of horse-riding in Iraq before the Kassite period', *Iraq* XXXII, 1970, 36–50; M.A. Littauer & J. Crouwel, *Wheeled Vehicles ...*, 66–8.

55 For a brilliant portrayal of one aspect of this invented tradition, R. Jenkyns, *The Victorians and ancient Greece*, Oxford 1980.

56 J.H. Crouwel, *Chariots ... in Bronze Age Greece*, Amsterdam 1981, R. Drews, *The Coming of the Greeks*, Princeton 1988.

57 J.H. Crouwel, *Chariots ...*, 32–36; J.A. Sakellarikis, 'Das Kuppelgrab A von Archanes und das kretisch-mykenische Tieropferritual', *Praehist. Zeitsch.* 45, 1970, 185–219.

58 M.A. Littauer, 'The function of the yoke saddle in ancient harnessing', *Antiq.* XLII, 1968, 27–31.

59 To select from a voluminous bibliography, M. Ventris & J. Chadwick, *Documents in Mycenaean Greek*, 1959, 1973;

M. Lejeune, 'La civilisation Mycénienne et la guerre', in J.P. Vernant (ed) *Problèmes de la guerre en Grèce ancienne*; Paris/La Haye 1968, 31–51; W.F. Wyatt, 'The Indo-Europeanization of Greece', in G. Cardona *et al.* (edd) *Indo-European and Indo-Europeans*, Philadelphia 1970, 89–111; J.H. Crouwel, *Chariots . . .*, 1981; W. Messerschmidt, 'Der agäische Streitwagen', *Acta praehist. & Arch*, 20, 1988, 31–44; R. Drews, *The Coming of the Greeks*, 1989.

60 M. Bernal, review of Drews, *Antiq.* 64, 1990, 167–9.

61 R. Drews, *Coming of the Greeks*, 181.

62 An exception is J. Gernet's short essay, 'Note sur le char en Chine', in J.P. Vernant (ed) *Problèmes de la guerre . . .*, 1968, 309–12.

63 W. Watson, *Cultural frontiers in ancient East Asia*, Edinburgh 1971; M. von Dewall, *Pferd und Wagen in frühen China*, Bonn 1964; 'Der Wagen in der Frühzeit Chinas', in W. Treue (ed), *Achse, Rad und Wagen*, Göttingen 1986, 168–86; S. Piggott, 'Chariots in the Caucasus and in China', *Antiq.* XLVIII, 1974, 16–24; 'Chinese chariotry: an outsider's view', in P. Denwood (ed) *Arts of the Eurasian Steppelands*, London 1977, 32–51; W.P. Yetts, 'The horse: a factor in early Chinese history', *Eurasia Sept. Antiq.* IX, 1934, 231–55; A. Waley, 'The Heavenly Horses of Ferghana: a new view', *History Today*, V, 1955, 95–103; H.G. Creel, *The origins of statecraft in China I, The Western Chou Empire*, Chicago & London 1970, 262–75; E.L. Shaughnessy, 'Historical perspectives on the introduction of the chariot into China', *Harvard Journ. Asiatic Studies* 48, 1988, 189–237.

64 S. Piggott, *EWT*, 91–92; M.A. Littauer, 'Rock carvings of chariots in Transcaucasia, Central Asia and Outer Mongolia', *Proc. Prehist. Soc.* 43, 1977, 243–62.

65 S.I. Rudenko (trans. M.W. Thompson), *Frozen Tombs of Siberia*, London 1970, 189–93.

66 S. Umehara, *Studies of Noin-ula finds in North Mongolia*, Tokyo 1960, xvii, fig.60; S.I. Rudenko, *Kultura chunnov i Noinulinskie kurgany*, Moscow 1962, 50.

67 M.A. Littauer, 'V.O. Vitt and the horses of Pazyryk', *Antiq.* LXV, 1971, 293–94.

68 A. Waley, *The Book of Songs*, London 1937, no.120. Waley notes (p.330) that his translation of the technical terms for harness are necessarily 'provisional'.

Chapter III (pp.69–122)

1 Quoted by R.H.C. Davis, 'The Medieval Warhorse', In F.M.L. Thompson (ed) *Horses in European economic history*, Reading 1983, 19; *The Medieval Warhorse*, London & New York 1989, 102.

2 J. Zarins, in *Equids*, 168; cf. Chap.II above.

3 P.R.S. Moorey, 'Pictorial Evidence . . .', *Iraq* XXXII, 1970, 36–50; M.A. Littauer & J.M. Crouwel, *Wheeled Vehicles . . .* 1979, 66–8.

4 Moorey, *loc. cit.*

5 Littauer & Crouwel, *loc. cit.*

6 A.L.F. Rivet, 'A note on scythed chariots', *Antiq.* LIII, 1979, 130–32.

7 Littauer & Crouwel, *Wheeled Vehicles . . .* 148, 155; M.A. Littauer, *Iraq* XXXIII, 1971, 24–30; L.F. Firouz, 'Osteological and historical implications of the Caspian miniature horse . . .' in J. Matolosi (ed) *Domestikationsforschung und Geschichte der Haustiere*, Budapest 1973, 309–15; 'The Caspian miniature horse of Iran', *Internat. Caspian Stud Book* II, 1978, 11–16.

8 N.K. Sandars, *The Sea Peoples*, London & New York 1978, 190.

9 M.I. Finley, 'Archaeology and the fall of Troy', *The Listener* Nov.7, 1963, 732–70.

10 J.K. Anderson, *Ancient Greek Horsemanship*, Berkeley & Los Angeles 1961.

11 Cf. J. Boardman, *The Greeks Over-*

seas, London & New York 1980, 165–68, 35–45.

12 S. Piggott, *Ancient Europe*, Edinburgh 1965, 176, 189, fig.106 (map); M.F. Vos, *Scythian archers in archaic Attic vase-painting*, Groningen 1963.

13 Translated text in Anderson, *loc. cit.*, 155–180.

14 T.G.E. Powell, 'The introduction of horse-riding to temperate Europe ...', *Proc. Prehist. Soc.* XXXVII, 1971, 1–14; J. Kastelic, *The Situla of Vače*, Belgrade 1956, 14, 15; Piggott, *EWT*, 180.

15 S. Bökönyi, *History of domestic mammals in Central and Eastern Europe*, Budapest 1974, 259–67; J.M.C. Toynbee, *Animals in Roman life and art*, London & New York 1973, 167–8; A. Hyland, *Equus: the horse in the Roman world*, London 1990.

16 Toynbee, *op. cit.* 169. Cf. P. Vigneron, *Le cheval dans l'antiquité Gréco-Romaine*, Nancy 1968, 235–314.

17 C.A. Burney & D.M. Lang, *The Peoples of the Hills*, London 1971, 129, 143; J.K. Anderson, *Ancient Greek horsemanship*, 30.

18 E. Delebecque, *Le cheval dans l'Iliade*, Paris 1951, 146; J.M.C. Toynbee, *Animals* ..., 177–81.

19 W. Groenman-van Waateringe, *Romaeinslederwerk uit Valkenburgh Z.H.*, Groningen 1967, 106–21; H. Russell Robinson, *The armour of Imperial Rome*, London 1975, 194–5.

20 S.I. Rudenko, *Frozen Tombs* ..., Chap.6; P. Vigneron, *Le cheval* ..., 83–4.

21 M.A. Littauer, 'Early stirrups', *Antiq.* LVI, 1981, 99–105; Lefebvre des Noettes, *L'Attelage et le cheval de selle*, 234, Pls.282–8; R.H.C. Davis, *Medieval warhorse*, fig.6.

22 Davis, *op. cit.* 14; for Rabanus, F.J.E. Raby, *Hist. Christian Latin poetry*, Oxford 1953, 179–83.

23 J.M.C. Toynbee, *Animals* ..., 169–71; Arrian, *Taktika*, 32–4; Chap.34 trans. in J. Curle, *A Roman frontier post* ..., Glasgow 1911, 172–173; H. Russell Robinson, *Armour of Imperial Rome*, 107–35 (parade helmets), 190–94 (chamfrons).

24 Procopius, *History of the Wars*, Book 8. Quoted in translation in A. Dent, *The Horse* ..., London 1974, 96–8; cf. S. Piggott, *Ancient Europe* 1965, 240 (with Arrian).

25 L.B. Vlad *et al*, 'The stylistic problems of the horses of San Marco' in *The Horses of San Marco* (Royal Academy/ Olivetti Exhib.), London 1979, 15–40; A.C. Levi, *Barbarians on Roman Imperial coins and sculpture* (Amer. Numis. Soc.), New York 1952; Benedict, *Mirabilia Urbis Romae* (*c*.1140), 41; D. Whitehouse, *Antiq.* LVII, 1983, 39.

26 H.P. Eydoux, *La France antique*, Paris 1962, 270; W. Krämer, *Germania* 67, 1989, 519–39; J.M.C. Toynbee, *Antiq. Journ.* XLIII, 1963, 264–8.

27 Lynn White Jr., *Medieval technology and social change*, Oxford 1962, 58.

28 J. Taeger, *Der reitende Papst*, Munich & Zurich 1970.

29 The dispute was prompted by Lynn White Jr., *Medieval technology and social change*, 1962. Among the main contributions have been P.H. Sawyer & R.H. Hilton, 'Technical determinism: the stirrup and the plough', *Past and Present* 24, 1963, 90–100; B.S. Bachrach, 'Charles Martel, mounted shock combat, the stirrup and feudalism', *Studies in Med. & Renaissance Hist.* VII, 1970, 49–75; R.H.C. Davis, *Medieval Warhorse*, 11–16; M.A. Littauer, 'Early stirrups', *Antiq.* LV, 1981, 99–105.

30 Lynn White, *Medieval technology* ..., 57–8; B.S. Bachrach *loc. cit.*, 59, 62; Davis, *Medieval Warhorse*, 77–8; S. Piggott, *Ancient Europe*, 252; *EWT*, 215–17; *Antiq.* XXII, 1948, 21–8.

31 Lynn White Jr., *Medieval religion and technology*, Los Angeles & London 1978, 228.

32 J. Langdon, *Horses, oxen and technological innovation*, Cambridge 1986.

33 P. Vigneron, *Le cheval* ..., 130–37 (classical); A.C. Leighton, *Transport and communication in early medieval Europe*, Newton Abbot 1972, 104 (medieval).

34 J.D. Muhly, 'Copper and tin', *Trans. Connecticut Acad. Arts & Sciences*, 43, 1973, 155–335 (trade); Littauer & Crouwel, *Wheeled Vehicles* ..., 66 (sealing).

35 Vigneron, *Le cheval* ..., 134; Toynbee, *Animals* ..., 197–9.

36 P. Vouga, *La Tène*, Leipzig 1923, 96–8, Pl.XXXV.

37 Lefebvre des Noettes, *L'Attelage* ..., 266–71.

38 E. Gibbon, *Decline and fall* ..., Chap.XI.

39 Toynbee, *Animals* ... , 240.

40 S. Piggott, *Ancient Europe*, 104–06; C.B.M. McBurney, 'Early man in the Soviet Union', *Proc. Brit. Acad.* LXI, 1975, 171–221, Pl.XV; E.H. Minns, 'Art of the northern nomads', *Proc. Brit. Acad.* XXVIII, 1942, 10.

41 Convenient illustrations in G.M.A. Richter, *Handbook of Greek Art*, London 1959, figs.113, 216, 206.

42 Martial, Ep.XIV.86, quoted by Vigneron, *Le cheval* ..., 83.

43 W. Lucke & O.H. Frey, *Der Situla in Providence*, Berlin 1962, Pls.14, 63 (Arnoaldi), 17, 64 (Certosa), 47, 48, 55, 73 (Vače), J. Kastelic, *Situlenkunst*, Vienna & Munich 1964, Pls.2, 3, 5 (Vače situla), 23 (Certosa), 50, 51 (Arnoaldi), 64–67 (Vače belt-plate).

44 M.F. Vos, *Scythian archers* ... The Pontic gold and silver work from Kul' Oba, Chertomlyk, Solokha and Ordzhonikidze with portrayals of Scythians is published in all books on Scythian art.

45 T.G.E. Powell, *Proc. Prehist. Soc.* XXXVII, 1971, 1–14 (Agighiol and Hallstatt scabbard); Letnitsa, I. Venedikov, *Les trésors de L'art de terres Bulgares*, Sofia 1965; *Thracian treasures from Bulgaria* (B.M. Exhib) 1976, nos.271–88; R.F. Hoddinott, *The Thracians*, London & New York 1981, 108–09, figs.158–61; E. Moscalu, 'Das Thrako-getische Fürstengrab von Perutu', *Bericht R.G. Komm.* 70, 1989, 129–90 (Agighiol and dating).

46 Powell, *loc. cit.*; R. & V. Megaw, *Celtic Art*, London & New York 1989, 80–81.

47 S.I. Rudcnko, *Frozen Tombs*, Pl.154 (poor colour drawing); M. Griaznov, *L'Art ancien de l'Altai*, Leningrad 1958, Pl.57 (best monochrome); M.J. Artamanov, 'Frozen tombs of the Scythians', *Scientific American*, 1965, 111 (direct colour but reversed).

48 Russell Robinson, *Armour of Imperial Rome*, 429–32 (Julius Caesar, Augustus, Drusus).

49 J.P. Wild, 'Clothing in the north-west provinces of the Roman empire', *Bonner Jahrb.* 168, 1968, 116–240.

50 Cf. K. Schumacher, *Germanendarstellungen*, R.G. Mus. Mainz, 1935.

51 S. Piggott, 'An ancient Briton from North Africa', *Antiq.* XLII, 1968, 128–30 with refs.

52 M. Todd, *The northern barbarians*, Oxford 1987, figs.28, 29; M. Hald, *Jernalderens Dragt*, Nat. Mus. Copenhagen, 1962.

53 *De Carolo Magno*, trans. with comment by Lewis Thorpe, *Einhard and Notker the stammerer*, Harmondsworth 1969. Quotations from Book I.34.

54 J.P. Wild, *loc. cit.*, 184.

55 J.P. Wild, *loc. cit.*, 221.

56 Lynn White Jr., *Medieval religion and technology*, Berkeley & London, 273.

57 John Evelyn, *Diary*, 13 Oct. 1666. The fashion was not a success.

58 J. Hackett, 'Reflections upon epic warfare', *Proc. Classical Assoc.* LXVIII, 1971, 13–32.

59 A.M. Snodgrass, *Arms and Armour of the Greeks*, London & New York 1967, 11.

60 F. Stenton (ed), *The Bayeux Tapestry*, London 1957, Pls.70–72.

61 A.M. Snodgrass, *Arms and Armour* ..., 1967; 'The first European body-armour', in J. Boardman *et al.* (ed), *The European community in later prehistory*, London 1971, 33–50.

62 Russell Robinson, *Armour Imp. Rome*, 147–52.

63 For the site, S. Lloyd, *Archaeology*

of Mesopotamia, London & New York 1978, 176–8.

64 Y. Yadin, *Art of warfare* ..., 84–5; Russell Robinson, *Oriental armour*, London 1967, 1–4.

65 E.H. Minns, *Scythians and Greeks*, Cambridge 1913, 73–4 and *passim*; R. Rolle, *The world of the Scythians*, London 1989, 67–9.

66 R.F. Hoddinott, *The Thracians*, 108–09, figs.158–61; *Thracian treasures*, nos.271–88.

67 Russell Robinson, *Armour Imp. Rome*, 153–61.

68 Russell Robinson, *Oriental armour*; A.D.H. Bivar, 'Cavalry equipment and tactics on the Euphrates frontier', *Dumbarton Oaks Papers* 26, 1972, 273–91; A. Hyland, *Equus* ..., 145–59.

69 Polybius VI.23.15, quoted by Bivar, *loc. cit.*, 276.

70 Varro, *De lingua latina* V.24; Diodorus Siculus V.30: *siderous halusidotous*, J.J. Tierney, 'The Celtic ethnography of Posidonius', *Proc. Roy. Irish. Acad.* 60 C, 1960, 189–275.

71 M. MacGregor, *Proc. Prehist. Soc.* XXVIII, 1962, 28 amending list in S. Piggott, *Proc. Soc. Ant. Scot.* LXXXVII, 1952–53, 39–40.

72 Minns, *Scythians and Greeks*, 174–6; Sulimirski, *Sarmatians*, 127.

73 M. Rusu & O. Bandula, *Das keltische Fürstengrab von Cumesti*, Baia Mare 1970.

74 P. Benedik *et al.*, *Keltische Gräberfelder der Sudwestslovakei*, Bratislava 1957, 32, 125.

75 G. Rosenberg, *Hjortspringfundet*, Copenhagen 1937; C.J. Becker, *Acta Arch.* XIX, 1948, 145–87.

76 I.M. Stead, *Excavations at Burton Fleming, Rudston, Garton-on-the-Wolds and Kirburn* (Eng. Heritage Arch. Reports) 1991.

77 T.G.E. Powell, *The Celts*, London & New York 1980, Pl.88.

78 M. Todd, *Northern barbarians*, 155, 158.

79 A.C. Evans, *The Sutton Hoo Ship Burial*, London 1986, 41; Davis, *Medieval Warhorse*, figs.23, 3.

80 J. Mann, 'Arms and armour' in F. Stenton (ed), *The Bayeux Tapestry*, 58–60.

81 Davis, *Medieval Warhorse*, 51.

82 Text & trans. in S. Bachrach, 'Charles Martel ...', 61; L. Thorpe, *Einhard and Notker*, 163.

83 J. Déchelette, *Manuel d'Archéologie* IV, 1927, 708–10; H. de S. Shortt, *Antiq. Journ.* XXXIX, 1959, 61–76.

84 Russell Robinson, *Oriental armour*, 84–5.

85 L. Thorpe, *Einhard and Notker*, 147.

86 William Fitzstephen, *Descriptio civitatis Londoniae*; text printed in J. Stow, *Survey of London* 1603; T. Hearne, *Leland's Itinerary* VIII.3. (1769 ed., pp.37–48); text and trans. in A. Dent & D.M. Goodall, *The foals of Epona*, London 1962, 97–8.

87 *Vita Sancti Thomae*, ed. J.C. Robertson, *Materials for the history of Thomas Becket*, Rolls Series III, 1877, Cap.119, p.122. Cf. Virgil, *Georgics* III, 79–88.

88 Davis, *Medieval Warhorse*, 21, 23; M. Jankovich, *They rode into Europe*, London 1971, 156. A Roman cavalryman's equipment has been estimated at 38.5 kg (85 lb); A. Hyland, *Equus* ... 1990, 154.

89 J.M.C. Toynbee, *Animals* ... Chap.II; L. Thorpe, *Einhard and Notker*, 149, 195; A. Leighton, *Transport and communication* ..., 31–2.

90 E.H. Gombrich, *Art and illusion*, New York 1960, 78.

91 *Byskupa Sögur*, ed. G. Jónsson, I, Reykjavik 1949. I am grateful to Mr Magnus Magnusson for this reference.

92 Pegolotti, *Pratica della mercatura* (1335–1343); H. Yule & H. Cordier, *Cathay and the way thither*, London 1866, III, 143–71; C.G.F. Simkin, *The traditional trade of Asia*, Oxford 1968, 135.

93 R. Grousset, *L'empire des steppes*, Paris 1960, 215, 282; Yule & Cordier, *Cathay* ..., II, 309–394, C. Dawson, *The Mongol Mission*, London 1955, xxxiii. I am grateful for help from the

Notes

94 B. Davidson, *Which way Africa?*, London 1964, 34; J. Needham, *Clerks and craftsmen in China and the West*, Cambridge 1970, 50.

95 T. Keegan, *The Heavy Horse*, London 1973, 13–21.

96 R. Thapar, *A history of India*, I, Harmondsworth 1966, 149, 208; Marco Polo, *The Travels*, trans. R. Latham, Harmondsworth 1958, 264.

97 A. Burnes, *Travels into Bokhara ... in the years 1831, 32 and 33*, London 1834, Chap.VI; J. Lunt, ' "Bokhara" Burnes', *History Today*, XIV, 1964, 665–77.

98 P.-M. Duval, *Les dieux de la Gaule*, Paris 1957, 46–8; J. de Vries, *La religion des Celtes*, Paris 1963, 132–4; A. Ross, *Pagan Celtic Britain*, London 1967, 224–5, 322–5; J.M.C. Toynbee, *Animals ...*, 1973, 197–9; A.L.F. Rivet & C. Smith, *Place-names of Roman Britain*, London 1979, 360–62.

99 P. Lambrechts, *Contributions à l'étude des divinités celtiques*, Bruges 1942, 81–99.

100 See n.26 above.

101 R.F. Hoddinott, *Thracians*, 169–75; G. Kazarow, 'The Thracian Rider and St George', *Antiq.* XII, 1938, 290–96.

102 H.E. Davidson, *Gods and myths of northern Europe*, Harmondsworth 1964, 97–8, 121–2; *Pagan Scandinavia*, London & New York 1967, 90–91.

103 S. Piggott, ' "Royal Tombs" reconsidered', *Prace i Materialy Mus. Arch. Lodz* 25, 1978, 293–301.

104 S. Piggott, 'Heads and Hoofs', *Antiq.* XXXVI, 1962, 110–18; N.K. Chadwick, *Poetry and prophecy*, Cambridge 1952, Pl.3.

105 S. Piggott, 'Nemeton, temenos, bothros: sanctuaries of the ancient Celts', *Accad. Nat dei Lincei*, Quad.237, 1978, 37–54; D.W. Harding, *Iron age in the upper Thames basin*, Oxford 1972, 70; *Hillforts*, London & New York 1976, 143; H. Jankuhn, 'Zur deutung der Tierknochenfunde aus La Tène', in R.

Degen *et al.* (edd) *Helvetia Antiqua*, Zurich 1966, 155–8.

106 S.I. Rudenko, *Frozen Tombs*, 1970, 40–42.

107 M.P. Gryaznov, *Arzhan: tsarskiy kurgan ranneskifskogo vremeni*, Leningrad 1980; 'Horses for the hereafter', *Unesco Courier* December 1976, 38–41; R. Rolle, *The world of the Scythians*, London 1989, 38–44.

108 Shandong Arch. Inst, 'Excavation of Eastern Zhou tomb ...' *Wen Wu* 9, 1984, 14 (Chinese); 'Rare sacrificial horse pit', *China Reconstructs* XXXIII, 9, Sept.1984, 59. I am grateful to Mrs M.A. Littauer for these references.

109 R. Rolle, *World of the Scythians*, 45–6.

110 M. Müller-Wille, 'Pferdegrab und Pferdeopfer im frühen Mittelalter', *Bericht Rijks. Oudheid. Bodemond.* 20–21, 1970–1971, 119–248.

111 E. James, *The Franks*, Oxford 1989, 62–3 with ref. Cf. J. Werner, 'Frankish royal tombs ...', *Antiq.* XXXVIII, 1964, 201–16.

112 W.B. Emery, *The royal tombs of Ballana and Qustul*, Cairo 1938; *Nubian treasure*, London 1948.

113 S. Bökönyi, *Hist. domesticated mammals in Central and Eastern Europe*, Budapest 1974, 268–9.

114 K. Thomas, *Man and the natural world*, London 1983, 115–16.

115 Giraldus Cambrensis, *Topographia Hiberniae*, III.25; M.J. Sjoestedt, *Dieux et héros des Celtes*, Paris 1940, xiv–xvi; M. Dillon & N. Chadwick, *The Celtic realms*, London 1967 (1973 ed), 126.

116 S. Bökönyi, *Hist. domestic mammals ...*, 290–92.

117 E.H. Tòth *et al.* 'The equestrian grave of Izsàk-Balaázspuszta ...', *Cumania (Archaeology)* IV, Kecsemét Mus. 1976, 141–211.

118 M. Eliade, *Shamanism: archaic techniques of ecstasy*, London 1964, 4, 190–98, 277; M.A. Czaplicka, *Aboriginal Siberia*, Oxford 1914, 198; N.K. Chadwick, *Poetry and prophecy*, Cambridge 1952, 76.

173

119 J. Innes Miller, *The spice trade of the Roman Empire*, Oxford 1969, 140–41; C.G.F. Simkin, *The traditional trade of Asia*, Oxford 1968.

120 Translated text, M. Müller-Wille, 'Pferdegrab ...', 182 (German); J.A. Boyle, 'The thirteenth-century Mongols' conception of the after life ...', *Mongolian Studies* (Amer. Mongolia Soc), I, 1974, 5–14 (English). The passage is omitted from the English translation in C. Waddy & H.L. Lorimer, 'A Scandinavian cremation-ceremony', *Antiq.* VIII, 1934, 58–62.

121 R. Grousset, *L'empire des steppes*, 241, 334, 342; C.G.F. Simkin, *Traditional trade ...*, 132–3.

122 Translated text in C. Dawson (ed), *The Mongol mission*, London & New York 1955, 12–13.

123 C. Dawson, *Mongol mission*, 105.

124 M.R.B. Shaw (trans. & ed.), *Joinville and Villehardouin: Chronicles of the Crusades*, Harmondsworth 1963, 290.

125 H.A.R. Gibbs (trans. & ed.), *Ibn Battuta, travels in Asia and Africa*, London 1929, 299–300.

Chapter IV (pp. 123–163)

1 J.G. Frazer, *The Golden Bough*, Chap.XXIV.2.

2 J. Thirsk, *Horses in early modern England: for service, for pleasure, for power*. Univ. Reading Stenton Lecture 1977, Reading, 1978; R.H.C. Davis, *The Medieval Warhorse*, London & New York 1989.

3 For Fitzstephen, above Chap.III, note 86.

4 Davis, *Medieval Warhorse*, 110–23.

5 John Aubrey, Wiltshire Collections 1659, The Country Revel, Life of Richard Corbet 1656; A. Powell, *Brief lives and other selected writings by John Aubrey*, London 1949, 10, 288.

6 S. Piggott, 'Copper vehicle-models in the Indus Civilization', *Journ. Royal Asiatic Soc.* 1970, 200–202; A.S. Gail,

'Der Wagen in Indien', in W. Treue, *Achse Rad und Wagen* 1986, 153–67.

7 J. Macintosh, 'Representation of furniture ... from Poggio Civitate (Murlo)', *Mitt. Deutsch. Arch. Inst. Röm.* 81, 1974, 15–40.

8 J. Traeger, *Der reitende Papst*, 1970.

9 J. Needham & G.Dj. Lu, 'Efficient equine harness: the Chinese inventions', *Physis* II.4. 1960, 121–62; M. von Dewall in W. Treue, *Achse Rad und Wagen* 1986, 179–80. House models, W. Watson, *Cultural Frontiers of ancient East Asia*, Edinburgh 1971, Pls.66, 67.

10 *Antiq.* LV, 1981, 105.

11 M.A. Littauer, *Proc. Prehist. Soc.* 43, 1977, 249, figs.20, 21.

12 S.I. Rudenko, *Frozen Tombs*, 183–93, Pls.129, 131, 166; M.P. Gryaznov, *South Siberia*, London 1969, Pls.80, 82, 83 (best photos); *Frozen Tombs* (B.M. Exhib. Cat.) 1978, nos.34–5 (swans).

13 A. Cotterell, *The First Emperor of China*, Harmondsworth 1981, 50–52. Number of spokes estimated from published photo.

14 S. Piggott, *EWT*, 1983, 187–90, fig.116.

15 The material up to 1981 was summarized with bibliography in S. Piggott, *EWT* 1983, 138–94; completely new survey in F.E. Barth *et al.*, *Vierrädige Wagen der Hallstattzeit*, Mainz 1987, with full documentation and outstanding illustrations; J. Biel, *Der Keltenfürst von Hochdorf*, Stuttgart 1985; C. Schovsbo, *Oldtidens vogne i Norden*, Bangsbo Mus. 1987.

16 M.N. Boyer, 'Medieval pivoted axles', *Technology & Culture* I, 1960, 128–38; cf. C.R. Hall 'More on medieval pivoted axles', ibid. II, 1961, 17–21.

17 S. Piggott, *EWT*, 156–58, quoting G. Jenkins, *The English Farm Wagon*, 101–102.

18 J.G. Jenkins, *Agricultural transport in Wales*, Cardiff 1962, 21–3; F. Galhano, *O carro de bois em Portugal*, Lisbon 1973.

19 L. Tarr, *The history of the carriage*, London 1969, fig.229, p.182.

20 R.H. Lane, 'Waggons and their ancestors', *Antiq.* IX, 1935, 140–50, Pl.III from BL MS Cotton Tib.v.f.6.

21 M. von Dewall, in W. Treue, *Achse Rad und Wagen*, 168–86; J. Needham & G.Dj. Lu, 'Efficient equine harness …', *Physis*, II.2., 121–62; VII.1., 1965, 70–4; Lynn White, *Medieval technology and social change* 1962, 61, Pl.3.

22 R.W. Bulliet, *The camel and the wheel*, 1975, 197–204; J.M.C. Toynbee, *Animals in Roman life …*, 176, figs.83, 85; A.C. Leighton, *Transport and communication …*, illus.149, 150 (Roman); J. Langdon, *Horses, oxen and technological innovation* 14, fig.5 (medieval).

23 P. Deffontaines, 'Sur la repartition … des voitures', *Cong. Internat. Folklore Paris 1937*, Tours 1938, 117–21; A.G. Haudricourt, 'Contribution de la géographie … de la voiture', *Rev. Géog. Humaine & d'Ethn.* 1948, 54–64; G. Jenkins, *English Farm Wagon*, 43–6, map fig.10.

24 Needham & Lu, 'Efficient equine harness', 132, fig.7; Strabo IV.1.14; VII.2.3; S. Piggott, *EWT*, 234.

25 J.M.C. Toynbee, *Animals in Roman Life …*, 186, Pl.89; W. Weber, 'Der Wagen in Italien und in den Römischen Provinzen', in W. Treue, *Achse Rad und Wagen*, 85–108; 96, 100.

26 L. Tarr, *History of the carriage*, figs.242, 243, 244, 251; W.H. Pyne, *Microcosm, or a picturesque delineation …*, London 1802–1808 (reprinted as *Picturesque views of rural occupations …*, New York 1977).

27 H. Haupt, 'Der Wagen im Mittelalter', in W. Treue, *Achse Rad und Wagen*, 187–96, quoting Otloh, *Vita Sancti Wolfgangi*, Cap.26 (p.194).

28 J. Langdon, *Horses, oxen and technological innovation*, Cambridge 1986, 142–57, esp.152.

29 O. Schovsbo, *Oldtidens vogne …*, fig.57; D. Wilson & O. Klindt-Jensen, *Viking Art*, London 1966, Pl.XIXa.

30 Lynn White Jr., 'The origins of the coach', *Medieval religion and technology*, Berkeley & London 1978, 205–216.

31 L. Tarr, *History of the carriage*, 183; all three vehicles are illustrated by Lefebvre des Noëttes, *L'Attelage …*, 125, fig.151; *Sol* with whipple-tree A. Leighton, *Transport and communication …*, fig.5; J. Langdon, *Horses …*, fig.6.

32 E.M. Stratton, *The World on Wheels*, New York 1878, reprinted 1972, 213–214, 258–9. I am grateful to Mrs Littauer for introducing me to this source, which though a century old contains much valuable information even if deficient of references at times.

33 William Fitzstephen, *Vita Sancti Thomae*, in J.C. Robertson (ed) *Materials for the history of Thomas Becket* (Rolls Series III), 1877, 29–33 (Cap.19). I am most grateful to the late Professor R.H.C. Davis for this fascinating reference.

34 Cf. Virgil, Georg. III, 536: *stridentes plaustra?*

35 E.M. Stratton, *World on Wheels*, 258.

36 L. Tarr, *History of the carriage*, 169 without further documentation.

37 J.F. Willard, 'Inland transportation in England during the fourteenth century', *Speculum* I, 1926, 361–74; 'The use of carts in the fourteenth century', *History* XVII, 1932–33, 246–50.

38 R.H. Wackernagel, 'Zur Geschichte der Kutsche bis zum Ende des 17 Jahrhunderts', in Treue, *Achse Rad und Wagen*, 197–235.

39 L. White, *loc. cit.* no.30 above; Tarr *loc. cit.*, Pl.XLIV; Haupt *loc. cit.* n.27, 190. I am grateful to Mr Martin Kauffmann of the Bodleian Library and to Mr Arthur MacGregor for help here.

40 Ebsdorf, Haupt p.196; St Denis, Lefebvre des Noëttes, *L'Attelage*, fig.154, E.M. Jope, 'Vehicles and harness' in C. Singer *et al.* (edd) *History of Technology*, II, Oxford 1956, 537–62; Toggenburg, J. Zemp, *Die Schweizerischen Bilderchroniken und ihre Architektur-Darstellungen*, Zürich 1879, fig.5; M.N. Boyer, *Technology and culture* I, 130; St Elizabeth, Tarr, *History of the carriage*,

Pl.XLV; Jean le Tavernier, Wackernagel in Treue, *Achse Rad und Wagen*, 201; Froissart, Tarr *op. cit.*, fig.230.

41 The Luttrell carriage has been frequently reproduced but the best (in colour) is J. Backhouse, *The Luttrell Psalter*, British Library, London 1989, 60–61. The heraldic device, if not purely decorative, is the arms of Speke or Speake of Somerset: the Luttrells had a Somerset branch of the family. I am indebted to Mr Thomas Woodcock, Somerset Herald, for this information.

42 Tarr, *History of the carriage*, Pls.XLII, L, figs.248, 249; Wackernagel *loc. cit.*, 200, 204.

43 C.H. Ward-Jackson & D.E. Harvey, *The English Gypsy caravan*, Newton Abbot 1972.

44 Wackernagel *loc. cit.*, 211.

45 *OED s.vv.*; Stratton *op. cit.*, 259.

46 J. Langdon, *Horses* ..., 151, 155 n. Wycliffe about 1400 translates the Vulgate *plaustrum* as *wayne*.

47 Tarr, *History of the carriage*, 203–08.

48 Lynn White, 'The origins of the coach', *op. cit.*, 217, fig.15; D.J.M. Smith, *A Dictionary of Horse-Drawn vehicles*, London 1988, 47.

49 Set out in 1878 by Stratton *op cit.*, 262, 270.

50 J. Stow, *The Annales ... of England* (1615), 867, quoted by Stratton *op. cit.*, 265; J. Thirsk, *Horses in early modern England* ..., 6.

51 John Strype, *Annals of the Reformation in England*, 1725–31 ed. III, 78, quoted by Stratton *op. cit.*, 266–7.

52 K. Thomas, *Man and the natural world*, 106.

53 J.M.C. Toynbee, *Animals in Roman life* ..., 104; H. Trevor-Roper, *Catholics, Anglicans and Puritans*, London 1987, 154.

54 J. Taylor, *The Worlde runnes on Wheeles*, 1623, quoted by Stratton *op. cit.*, 273–287; H. Peacham, *Coach and Sedan, pleasantly disputing for place and precedence* ..., 1636, quoted by Thirsk, *Horses in early modern England* ..., 6;

M. Drayton, *Ideas Mirrour* 1594, Sonnet vi.

55 *English Silver Treasures from the Kremlin*. Sotheby Exhibition Cat. 1991, esp. M.V. Unkovskaya, pp.27, 34; N. Siselina, pp.115–35.

56 N. Siselina *loc. cit.*, 116.

57 O. Neverov, 'His Majesty's Cabinet and Peter I's *Kunstkammer*' in O. Impey & A. MacGregor (edd) *The Origins of Museums*, Oxford 1985, 54–61.

58 Cf. D.W.J. Gill, *Antiq.* 62, 1988, 735–43; M. Vickers, *Amer. Journ. Arch.* 94, 1990, 613–25 and earlier studies by both authors.

59 V.G. Lukonin, *Persia II*, Geneva 1967, 215–26.

60 R. Hakluyt, *The Principall Navigations*, 1598, Hakluyt Soc. Facs. Ed. London 1965, 491. I am grateful to Mr Michael Strachan for this reference.

61 *Sir Thomas Smithes Voiage and Entertainments in Rushia*, London 1605; S. Purchas, *Purchas His Pilgrimes*, London 1625, Pt.III, vol.iv, 747–53, quoted here.

62 A pair of silver gilt flagons: *Sotheby Exhib. Cat.* 1991, no.94.

63 Photos, Wackernagel *loc. cit.*, 219; *Sotheby Exhib. Cat.*, 31, fig.5. Model, D. Wray, 'Mission to Moscow', *The Woodworker*, July 1983, 417–20; 'Boris Godunov's Coach', *The Carriage Journal* 23, 1985, 79–91. I am grateful to Mrs Littauer for originally drawing my attention to this model and to the staff of the Road Transport Collection of the Science Museum for subsequent help.

64 M. Watney, *Royal Cavalcade*, London 1987, 23. An amateurish work bereft of references but well illustrated.

65 M. Strachan, *Sir Thomas Roe 1581–1644: A Life*, Wilton 1989, and help from the author.

66 J.L. Cranmer-Byng, *An Embassy to China*, London 1962; M. Sahlins, 'Cosmologies of capitalism ...', *Proc. Brit. Acad.* LXXXIV, 1988, 1–51.

67 J. Needham, *Clerks and craftsmen in China and the West*, Cambridge 1970, esp. 1–13, 227–8.

68 W.B. Adams, *English Pleasure Carriages*, London 1837, repr. & ed. J. Simmons, Bath 1971; G.A. Thrupp, *A History of Coaches*, London 1877; E.M. Stratton, *The World on Wheels ...*, New York 1878, repr. New York 1972. D.J.M. Smith, *A Dictionary of Horse-Drawn Vehicles*, London 1988, is a guide through the maze of nomenclature.

69 D. Cannadine, 'The context, performance and meaning of ritual: British monarchy and the "Invention of Tradition", c.1820–1977', in E. Hobsbawm & T. Ranger, *The Invention of Tradition*, Cambridge 1983, 101–64.

70 *The Times*, 13 Jan. 1953, quoted by S. Piggott, *Ancient Europe*, 1965, 196; *The Times*, 20 May 1977.

Further Reading

The notes to the text document specific points, but a selection may be made of general works likely to help the reader.

Two general books on wheeled transport in antiquity are S. Piggott, *The Earliest Wheeled Transport* (London & New York 1983) and M.A. Littauer & J. Crouwel, *Wheeled Vehicles in the Ancient Near East* (Leiden 1979). A good popular account is L. Tarr, *The History of the Carriage* (London 1969), and (in German) the 15 essays from prehistory to recent times collected in W. Treue (ed), *Achse, Rad und Wagen* (Göttingen 1986).

For horses, valuable conference papers are collected in R.H. Meadows & H.P. Uepman (edd), *Equids in the Ancient World* (Wiesbaden 1986); A. Hyland, *Equus: the Horse in the Roman World* (London 1990); J. Langdon, *Horses, Oxen and Technical Innovation* (Cambridge 1986); R.H.C. Davis, *The Medieval Warhorse* (London & New York 1989).

General topics are dealt with by J.P. Mallory, *In Search of the Indo-Europeans* (London & New York 1989); H. Russel Robinson, *The Armour of Imperial Rome* (London 1979); R. Rolle, *The World of the Scythians* (London 1989); C. Dawson, *The Mongol Mission* (London & New York 1955).

Sources of Illustrations

Index